MEDIEVAL LEGENDS

Imitation in Writing Series
Book 6

Matt Whitling

Logos School Materials
Moscow, Idaho

Imitation In Writing

This Medieval Legends text is the sixth book in a growing series of Imitation in Writing materials designed to teach aspiring writers the art and discipline of crafting delightful prose and poetry.

Aesop's Fables
Fairy Tales
Greek Myths
Greek Heroes
Medieval Legends
The Grammar of Poetry

C084 Imitation in Writing - Medieval Legends
ISBN 1-930443-68-4   20.00

Logos School Materials
110 Baker Street, Moscow, Idaho 83843
Toll Free 866-562-2174
www.logosschool.com or logosschool@turbonet.com

Call, write, or email for a free catalog of our Classical,
Christian educational materials for schools and home schools.

CONTENTS

Imitation In Writing
MEDIEVAL LEGENDS

<u>Background:</u>

We are commanded in Scripture to imitate the Lord Jesus Christ. We are also commanded to imitate those brothers and sisters who, through faith and patience, have inherited the promises. To imitate something or someone means:

- To do or try to do after the manner of; to follow the example of; to copy in action.
- To make or produce a copy or representation of; to copy, reproduce.
- To be, become, or make oneself like; to assume the aspect or semblance of; to simulate.

This God-sanctioned method of learning is an essential tool for educating young people. For example, how is it that we teach a child to perform simple physical skills such as throwing and catching? "Hold your hands **like this**. Step forward as you throw **like this**." Imitation. How is it that we teach a child how to form his letters correctly? "Hold your pencil **like this**. Look at **this 'a'**. Trace **this letter**. Now, you try to make an 'a' **like this one**." Imitation. How is it that we teach art? At Logos School students learn how to paint by imitating master painters of the past. "**This** is a good painting. Let's see if you can **reproduce it**." Imitation. How is it that music is taught, or reading, or math? Very often the best instruction in any of these areas necessarily includes imitation. Why, when it comes to teaching young people writing, do we educators regularly neglect this effective tool?

Educators in seventeenth century England knew the value of imitation as a tool through which they could teach style, particularly in the area of writing. The primary method of imitation in these English grammar schools was called *Double Translation*. In a double translation the teacher would translate a Latin work into English. The student was to copy this English translation over, paying close attention to every word and its significance. Then the student was to write down the English and Latin together, one above the other, making each language answer to the other. Afterwards the student translated the original Latin to English on his own. This was the first part of the translation. The second part took place ten days afterward when the student was given his final English translation and required to turn it back into good Latin.

Benjamin Franklin wrote of a similar exercise that he employed to educate himself a century later. When he was a young man, he came across a particular piece of writing that he delighted in, *The Spectator*. *The Spectator* is a series of 555 popular essays published in 1711 and 1712. These essays were intended to improve manners and morals, raise the cultural level of the middle-class reader, and popularize serious ideas in science and philosophy. They were written well, the style was excellent, and Franklin wanted to imitate it. Here is Franklin's method of "double translation" regarding *The*

Spectator:

> With that view (imitating this great work) I took some of the papers, and making short hints of the sentiments in each sentence, laid them by a few days, and then, without looking at the book, tried to complete the papers again, by expressing each hinted sentiment at length, and as fully as it had been expressed before, in any suitable words that should occur to me. Then I compared my Spectator with the original, discovered some of my faults, and corrected them.

But he realized that he needed a greater stock of words in order to add variety and clarity of thought to his writing.

> Therefore I took some of the tales in the Spectator, and turned them into verse; and, after a time, when I had pretty well forgotten the prose, turned them back again. I also sometimes jumbled my collection of hints into confusion, and after some weeks endeavored to reduce them into the best order, before I began to form the sentences and complete the subject. This was to teach me method in the arrangement of thoughts. By comparing my work with the original, I discovered many faults and corrected them; but I sometimes had the pleasure to fancy that, in particulars of small consequence, I had been fortunate enough to improve the method or the language, and this encouraged me to think that I might in time become to be a tolerable English writer, of which I was extremely ambitious.

Now the question is; "How can we employ a similar methodology?"

Imitation In Writing
MEDIEVAL LEGENDS

<u>Instructions:</u>

1. READ SILENTLY: Have the students read the legend quietly to themselves, paying close attention to the story line. When they are done, they should underline the vocabulary words and describe the characters. Discuss, by means of questioning, who the characters are in the legend and what took place.

2. STUDENT READS LEGEND: Choose a student to come to the front of the class and read the entire legend while the class follows along. *(Variation: To develop listening and note taking skills try reading the legend to your students without giving them a copy of it.)*

3. ORAL RETELLING: The teacher calls on individual students to retell the legend in their own words. These oral summaries should be short and to the point.

4. VOCABULARY: Call on one student for each of the vocabulary words. That student will read the sentence in which the word is found, providing context, and then define the word for the class. Occasionally the student definition will need to be modified by the teacher so that it is an exact match with the vocabulary word in the legend. One word definitions work well. The idea here is to provide the students with a synonym for each vocabulary word which could be substituted into the sentence without distorting the meaning. Have the students write the definition of each word on the blank provided.

5. OUTLINE THE PLOT: Initially this activity should be guided by the teacher and completed as a class. Providing every other simple sentence or phrase for each scene is helpful for younger students. There is some room for variation in the exact wording of the sentence or phrase. The rules are that each sentence or phrase must be three to four words long and represent a significant chronological event in that scene. From time to time the students will come up with a better sentence or phrase than the one provided in the Suggested Plot Summaries at the back of this book. Use it, by all means.

6. CHARACTERS: At this point the students will list the main characters in the story and write a few descriptive words about each.

7. ADDITIONAL REQUIREMENTS: Discuss any additional requirements and have the students write them on the blanks provided at the bottom of each worksheet. For examples of additional requirements see *EXCELLENCE IN WRITING* @ 800-856-5815 (stylistic techniques, dress-ups, sentence openers, etc...) or teach your students figures of speech and require that they use them in their own writing (metaphor, simile, synecdoche, hyperbole, onomatopoeia, rhetorical question, personification, pun, oxymoron, alliteration).

8. PASS IN ORIGINAL LEGEND: Before the students begin rewriting the legend, they must pass the original one in. Some students will want to read through the legend one more time to better understand what the whole thing is all about.

9. WRITE FIRST DRAFT: The students are now ready to rewrite the legend using their outlines to guide them. I allow my students to change the characters and some of the incidentals of the story in their rewrites as long as the plot is identifiable. The exceptionally good writers in the class will thrive off of this opportunity to be innovative. The students who are less comfortable with writing will tend to stick to the same characters and incidentals, which is fine. All of the vocabulary words must be used correctly and underlined in the rewrite. The students should skip lines on the first draft to allow room for editing.

10. PARENTS EDIT: Students take their rewrites home to complete the first draft and then they have their parents edit it. This is most profitable when the parents sit down with the student and edit the legend together. Guidelines for editing can be sent home at the beginning of the year or communicated at "Back to School Night" so that parents know what is expected.

11. FINAL DRAFT: Time in class can be provided for the students to work on the final draft. The students should not skip lines. I allow the students to draw an illuminated letter at the beginning of their story if they like.

12. GRADING: There is a grading sheet included which can be duplicated, cut out, completed, and stapled to each student's rewrite. This will help the teacher to focus on the essential aspects of the composition as he is grading it and will provide specific feedback to the student and parents regarding which areas will need more attention in the future. If you have a different policy for grading writing assignments then simply disregard the grading sheet.

MEDIEVAL LEGENDS

1st Draft / Worksheet	10	____
Handwriting	10	____
Vocab. Usage	20	____
Content (style, structure...)	30	____
Mechanics (spell, punct...)	30	____
Total	100	____

MEDIEVAL LEGENDS

1st Draft / Worksheet	10	____
Handwriting	10	____
Vocab. Usage	20	____
Content (style, structure...)	30	____
Mechanics (spell, punct...)	30	____
Total	100	____

MEDIEVAL LEGENDS

1st Draft / Worksheet	10	____
Handwriting	10	____
Vocab. Usage	20	____
Content (style, structure...)	30	____
Mechanics (spell, punct...)	30	____
Total	100	____

MEDIEVAL LEGENDS

1st Draft / Worksheet	10	____
Handwriting	10	____
Vocab. Usage	20	____
Content (style, structure...)	30	____
Mechanics (spell, punct...)	30	____
Total	100	____

MEDIEVAL LEGENDS

1st Draft / Worksheet	10	____
Handwriting	10	____
Vocab. Usage	20	____
Content (style, structure...)	30	____
Mechanics (spell, punct...)	30	____
Total	100	____

MEDIEVAL LEGENDS

1st Draft / Worksheet	10	____
Handwriting	10	____
Vocab. Usage	20	____
Content (style, structure...)	30	____
Mechanics (spell, punct...)	30	____
Total	100	____

Beowulf and Grendel

I

Hrothgar, King of Denmark, was a descendant of Odin. As he had amassed much wealth in the course of a long life of warfare, he resolved to devote part of it to the construction of a magnificent hall, called Heorot, where he might feast his retainers and listen to the heroic lays of the scalds during the long winter evenings.

The inauguration of this hall was celebrated by a sumptuous entertainment; and when all the guests had retired, the king's bodyguard, composed of thirty-two dauntless warriors, lay down in the hall to rest. When morning dawned and the servants appeared to remove the couches, they beheld with horror the floor and walls all stained with blood, the only trace of the knights who had gone to rest there in full armor.

Gigantic, blood-stained footsteps, leading directly from the festive hall to the sluggish waters of a deep mountain lake, or fiord, furnished the only clue to their disappearance. They had been made by Grendel, a descendant of the giants, whom a magician had driven out of the country, but who had evidently returned to renew his former depredations.

As Hrothgar was now too old to wield a sword with his former skill, his first impulse was, of course, to offer a princely reward to any man brave enough to free the country of this terrible scourge. As soon as this was known, ten of his doughtiest knights volunteered to camp in the hall on the following night and attack the monster Grendel should he venture to reappear.

But in spite of the valor of these experienced warriors and the efficacy of their oft-tried weapons, they too succumbed. A minstrel, hiding in a dark corner of the hall, was the only one who escaped Grendel's fury, and after shudderingly describing the massacre he had witnessed, he fled in terror to the kingdom of the Geates. There he sang his lays in the presence of Hygelac, the king, and of his nephew Beowulf (the Bee Hunter) and roused their deepest interest by describing the visit of Grendel and the vain but heroic defense of the brave knights. Beowulf, having listened intently, eagerly questioned the scald, and, learning from him that the monster still haunted those regions, impetuously declared his intention to visit Hrothgar's kingdom and show his valor by fighting and, if possible, slaying Grendel.

Although very young, Beowulf was quite distinguished and had already won great honors in a battle against the Swedes. Now he expressed a hope that he might prevail against Grendel and, embarking with fourteen chosen men, he sailed to Denmark, where he was challenged by the coast guard and warmly welcomed as soon as he had made his purpose known.

II

Hrothgar received Beowulf most hospitably but vainly tried to dissuade him from his perilous undertaking. Then, after a sumptuous banquet, where the mead flowed with true northern lavishness, Hrothgar and his suite sadly left the hall Heorot in charge of the brave band of strangers, whom they never expected to see again.

As soon as the king had departed, Beowulf bade his companions lie down and sleep in peace, promising to watch over them, yet laying aside both armor and sword; for he knew that weapons were of no avail against the monster whom he intended to grapple with hand to hand should it really appear.

The warriors had no sooner stretched themselves out upon the benches in the hall than, overcome by the oppressive air as well as by the mead, they sank into a profound sleep. Beowulf alone remained awake, watching for Grendel's coming. In the early morning, when all was very still, the giant appeared, tore asunder the iron bolts and bars which secured the door , and striding into the hall, enveloped in a long, damp mantle of clammy mist, he pounced upon one of the sleepers. He tore him limb from limb, greedily drank his blood, and devoured his flesh, leaving naught but the head, hands, and feet of his unhappy victim. This ghastly repast only whetted the fiend's ravenous appetite, however, so he eagerly stretched out his hands in the darkness to seize and devour another warrior. Imagine his surprise and dismay when he suddenly found his hand caught in so powerful a grasp that all his efforts could not wrench it free!

Grendel and Beowulf struggled in the darkness, overturning tables and couches, shaking the great hall to its very foundations, and causing the walls to creak and groan under the violence of their furious blows. But in spite of Grendel's gigantic stature, Beowulf clung so fast to the hand and arm he had grasped that Grendel, making a desperate effort to free himself by a jerk, tore the whole limb out of its socket! Bleeding and mortally wounded, he then beat a hasty retreat to his marshy den, leaving a long, bloody trail behind him.

As for Beowulf, exhausted but triumphant, he stood in the middle of the hall, where his companions crowded around him, gazing in speechless awe at the mighty hand and limb and the clawlike fingers, far harder than steel, which no power had hitherto been able to resist.

At dawn Hrothgar and his subjects also appeared. They heard with wonder a graphic account of the night's adventures and gazed their fill upon the monster's limb, which hung like a trophy from the ceiling of Heorot. After the king had warmly congratulated Beowulf and bestowed upon him many rich gifts, he gave orders to cleanse the hall, to hang it with tapestry, and to prepare a banquet in honor of the conquering hero.

III

When the banquet was ended, Hrothgar escorted his guests to more pleasant sleeping apartments than they had occupied the night before, leaving his own men to guard the hall, where Grendel would never again appear. The warriors, fearing no danger, slept in peace; but in the dead of night the mother of the giant, as gruesome and uncanny a monster as he, glided into the hall, secured the bloody trophy still hanging from the ceiling, and carried it away, together with Aeschere, the king's bosom friend.

When Hrothgar learned this new loss at early dawn, he was overcome with grief; and when Beowulf, attracted by the sound of weeping, appeared at his side, he mournfully told him of his irretrievable loss.

The young hero immediately volunteered to finish his work and avenge Aeschere by seeking and attacking Grendel's mother in her own retreat; but as he knew the perils of this expedition, Beowulf first gave explicit directions for the disposal of his personal property in case he never returned. Then, escorted by the Danes and Geates, he followed the blood track until he came to a cliff overhanging the waters of the mountain pool. There the bloody traces ceased, but Aeschere's gory head was placed aloft as a trophy.

Beowulf gazed down into the deep waters, saw that they also were darkly dyed with the monster's blood, and, after taking leave of Hrothgar, bade his men await his return for two whole days and nights ere they definitely gave him up for lost. He then plunged bravely into the bloody waters, swam about seeking for the monster's retreat, and dived deep. At last, descrying a phosphorescent gleam in the depths, he quickly made his way thither, shrewdly conjecturing that it must be Grendel's hiding place.

A strong current seized Beowulf and swept him irresistibly along into the slimy retreat of Grendel's mother. She clutched him fast, wrestled with him, deprived him of his sword, flung him down, and finally tried to pierce his armor with her trenchant knife. Fortunately, however, the hero's armor was weapon-proof and his muscles were so strong that before she could do him any harm he had freed himself from her grasp. Seizing a large sword hanging upon a projection of rock near by, he dealt her a mighty blow, severing her head from the trunk at a single stroke. The blood pouring out of the cave mingled with the waters without, and turned them to such a lurid hue that Hrothgar and his men sorrowfully departed, leaving the Geates alone to watch for the return of the hero, whom they feared they would never see again.

Beowulf, in the mean while, had rushed to the rear of the cave, where, finding Grendel in the last throes, he cut off his head also. He seized this ghastly trophy and rapidly made his way up through the tainted waters, which the fiery blood of the two monsters had so overheated that his sword melted in its scabbard and naught but the hilt remained.

The Geates were about to depart in sorrow, notwithstanding the orders they had received, when they suddenly beheld their beloved chief safe and sound and bearing the evidences of his success. Then their cries of joy echoed and reechoed from the neighboring hills, and Beowulf was escorted back to Heorot, where he was almost overwhelmed with gifts by the grateful Danes. A few days later Beowulf and his companions returned home, where the story of their adventures and an exhibition of all the treasures they had won formed the principal topics of conversation.

Beowulf & Grendel

Name: _____

I. Vocabulary: Underline the following words in the legend. Define each word and use it in a short sentence below.

○ lays: _____

○ impetuously: _____

○ repast: _____

○ phosphorescent: _____

○ trenchant: _____

II. Plot: Write a simple sentence or phrase to describe the main actions that take place in each scene.

News of Grendel	A Night in Heorot	Double Revenge
1. _____	1. _____	1. _____
2. _____	2. _____	2. _____
3. _____	3. _____	3. _____

III. Characters: List and briefly describe the main characters in this legend.

_____

_____

_____

IV. Rewrite this legend. Be sure to:

○ Include and underline all of the vocabulary words.

○ Write at least three separate paragraphs.

○ Include the following additional requirements.

11

Beowulf and the Firedrake

I

A long reign of comparative peace brought Beowulf to old age. He had naturally lost much of his former vigor and was, therefore, somewhat dismayed when a terrible, fire-breathing dragon took up its abode in the mountains near by, where it gloated over a hoard of glittering gold.

A fugitive slave, having made his way unseen into the monster's den during one of its temporary absences, bore away a great golden cup. On its return the Firedrake discovered the theft and became so furious that its howling and writhing shook the mountain like an earthquake. When night came on, its rage was still unappeased, and it flew all over the land, vomiting venom and flames, setting houses and crops afire, and causing so much damage that the people were almost beside themselves with terror. Seeing that all their attempts to appease the dragon were utterly fruitless and being afraid to attack it in its lair, they finally implored Beowulf to deliver them as he had delivered the Danes and to slay this oppressor which was even worse than the terrible Grendel.

II

Such an appeal could not be disregarded, and in spite of his advanced years Beowulf donned his armor once more and had a shield made of iron to withstand the flames of the beast. Accompanied by Wiglaf and eleven of his bravest men, he then went out to seek the monster in its lair. At the entrance of the mountain gorge Beowulf bade his followers pause and, advancing alone to the monster's den, he boldly challenged it to come forth and begin the fray. A moment later the mountain shook as the monster rushed out breathing fire and flame, and Beowulf felt the first gust of its hot breath, even through his massive shield.

A desperate struggle followed, in the course of which Beowulf's sword and strength both failed him. The Firedrake coiled its long, scaly folds about the aged hero and was about to crush him to death when the faithful Wiglaf, perceiving his master's imminent danger, sprang forward and attacked the monster so fiercely as to cause a diversion and make it drop Beowulf to concentrate its attention upon him.

Beowulf, recovering, then drew his dagger and soon put an end to the dragon's life; but even as it breathed its last, the hero sank fainting to the ground. Feeling that his end was near, he warmly thanked Wiglaf for his timely aid, rejoiced in the death of the monster, and bade his faithful follower bring out the concealed treasure and lay it at his feet, that he might feast his eyes upon the glittering gold he had won for his people's use.

III

The mighty treasure was all brought forth to the light of day, and the followers, seeing that all danger was over, crowded round their dying chief. He addressed them affectionately, and, after recapitulating the main events of his career, expressed a desire to be buried in a mighty mound on a projecting headland which could be seen far out at sea and would be called by his name.

These directions were all piously carried out by a mourning people who decked his mound with the gold he had won and erected above it a Bauta, or memorial stone, to show how dearly they had loved their brave king Beowulf, who had died to save them from the fury of the dragon.

Beowulf & the Firedrake

Name: _____

I. Vocabulary: Underline the following words in the legend. Define each word and use it in a short sentence below.

○ abode: _____
○ donned: _____
○ fray: _____
○ imminent: _____
○ recapitulating: _____

II. Plot: Write a simple sentence or phrase to describe the main actions that take place in each scene.

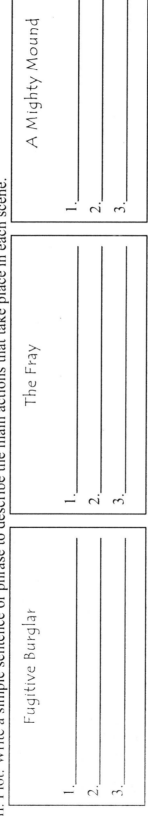

Fugitive Burglar

1. _____
2. _____
3. _____

The Fray

1. _____
2. _____
3. _____

A Mighty Mound

1. _____
2. _____
3. _____

III. Characters: List and briefly describe the main characters in this legend.

_____
_____
_____

IV. Rewrite this legend. Be sure to:

○ Include and underline all of the vocabulary words.
○ Write at least three separate paragraphs.
○ Include the following additional requirements.

○ _____
○ _____
○ _____

13

Young Roland – Part 1

I

Once summer afternoon rather more than eleven hundred years ago, the boy Roland was sitting in the cleft of a broken rock that forms the crest of one of the hills in the neighborhood of Sutri. Above him was the deep blue sky of Italy, on either side of him stretched a dull, uneven plain, broken here and there by wet marshes. A mile or more to the south could be seen the old town with its strong castle. Directly beneath him was the dusty highroad, which, after much winding, was lost to sight in a strip of dusky woodland a league and more to the northward. Along that road King Charlemagne, with the flower of his great army, was hourly expected to pass, marching on his way to the castle of Sutri, where he was to be entertained for a time as a guest; and it was for this reason that the lad sat so still and watched so long in his half-hidden perch on the hilltop.

Now and then the sound of voices from the town or the cries of the soldiers in the garrison came to Roland's ears. There he sat, waiting and wondering and anxiously watching for any sign of the coming host. The fair face of the lad and the long flaxen hair which fell in glistening waves upon his bare shoulders showed his kinship to the hardy races of the North. And there was something in the piercing look of his eye, in the proud curl of his lip, in the haughty turn of his head, which made him seem like a young king among men and which often had caused those who met him to doff the hat in humble courtesy. He was very poorly clad: his head and limbs were bare; and the thin, scant clothing which covered his body was nought but rags and shreds. Yet he bore himself proudly, as one who knew his own worth and who, having a blameless heart, had nothing of which to feel ashamed.

By and by another boy came over the crest of the hill and stood in the cleft of the rock by the side of Roland and with him gazed down the deserted road. He seemed of about the same age as Roland and, like him, was tall and sparely built. His dark hair and overhanging brows, his ruddy face and flashing eyes, betokened an equal kinship with the danger-daring North-folk and the leisure-loving people of the South. He wore the rich dress of a court page and carried himself with a lofty grace such as only those who bear brave hearts can ever show.

"I feared you were not coming, Oliver," said Roland, offering his hand but not once turning his head or taking his eyes from the distant woodland.

"It was indeed hard for me to get leave," answered the other. "But the ladies at the castle are very kind, and here I am.

II

"I think I see them coming now," said Roland. "There is a glimmering of light among the trees, which I think must be the flashing of the sun upon their armor."

He had scarcely finished speaking when the clear notes of a bugle were heard, borne faintly to them on the breeze. Presently the edge of the wood seemed ablaze with the flashing shields and glittering war coats. The boy Roland leaped to his feet. He stood on tiptoe and strained himself eagerly forward; his face beamed with delight; and his eyes sparkled with that strange wild fire which in after-days, in the midst of the battle's din, was wont to strike his foes with terror. Oliver climbed to the highest point of the rock and gazed with an eagerness, half mixed with fear, at the wonderful array of steel-clad warriors who now could be plainly seen issuing from the woodland.

The vanguard of the procession drew rapidly nearer. In front rode four and twenty knights, the heralds of the king, bearing aloft the silken banner of France and the golden eagle of Rome. They were clad in rich armor which glittered like gold in the sunlight; their shields were inlaid with many priceless gems and polished as bright as mirrors; and the sharp points of their long lances flashed around them like the restless gleams of lightning in the van of a summer storm-cloud. They were mounted on milk-white horses trapped with white cloth-of-gold, with gold-red saddles, and housings of bluest silk.

The boy Roland had never seen anything so beautiful or so grand, and he thought that one of these knights must surely be Charlemagne. And as they drew very near to the foot of the hill and he could look down almost upon the heads of the brilliant company, he called to Oliver, and asked,

"Which of these knights is the great Charles? Is it not he who rides nearest the standard-bearer? He, surely, is the noblest warrior of them all; and he rides with a grace which well becomes a king."

But this scene, which filled the mind of Roland with such astonishment, was not altogether new to Oliver.

"No," he answered. "The great king is not one of these. They are but heralds and messengers who ride before to my father's castle to see that everything is in readiness for their master.

Following the heralds came a body of guards, a thousand men of giant stature and muscles of iron, incased

14

from head to foot in strongest armor and riding heavy war-steeds trapped with steel. After these came a long line of bishops and abbots and monks and priests, most of them dressed in the garb of their office or profession and riding on the backs of palfreys or of mules.

Then the whole highway and the fields before them seemed filled with steel-coated men, and the horses clothed in steel trappings; and the long lances in the hands of the knights seemed as thick-set as the blades of grass in an autumn meadow. First and foremost in this company was Charlemagne himself, clad in steel from head to foot and riding a horse of the color of steel and the strength of steel. Roland, as soon as he saw him, knew that this must be the king. The noblest knight among his followers seemed but a weak stripling when seen by the side of the matchless Charlemagne.

With wonder, Roland kept his eyes fixed upon the noble figure of Charlemagne; and he did not withdraw his gaze until a sudden turn of the road around the hill toward Sutri hid the company from sight. He did not care to see that part of the host which followed. He had seen the great Charles, and that was all he wished. He beckoned to Oliver; and the two boys climbed down from their well-hidden lookout and started homeward.

By this time the short twilight was fast giving place to darkness. With hasty steps Roland made his way across the fields toward the little cave hollowed out of the rocky hillside that was home. Few were the comforts in this humble dwelling; and but for the kind welcome of his queen-like mother, the Lady Bertha, small would have been the cheer that Roland would have found there.

III

"I have seen him, mother!" he cried, rushing into her arms.

Then the gentle Bertha took the lad's hand in her own, and the two sat down together and Roland told her of all he had seen that memorable afternoon.

"And now, dear mother," said he, "the time has come for me to learn the great secret of my life. Today I am twelve years old and have seen Charlemagne; today you have promised to tell me about my kinsfolk and myself.

Then the Lady Bertha drew the lad close to her and told him the story of her own life and his. She told him how she, the spoiled and petted daughter of Pepin, had been brought up at the French court; and how, after her father's death, she had lived in her brother's kingly palace at Aix. Then she told how there came to Charlemagne's court a worthy knight named Milon, a warrior poor and needy but brave and without reproach.

"And when your mother, then the Princess Bertha, saw the gallant Count Milon and heard of his nobleness, she loved him. And your uncle Charlemagne hated him and banished him from France; for he wished to wed his sister to duke Ganelon of Mayence, one of his peers. But, when Milon fled from the king's court, he went not alone; he took me, the Princess Bertha, with him as his wife. The good Archbishop Turpin had secretly married us and given us his blessing and promised to help us on our way to Italy. When Charlemagne heard how he had been outwitted, he was very angry, and he swore that he would do his uttermost to ruin Count Milon and to bring me back to France. And so, to escape his anger, we dressed ourselves in the guise of beggars and wandered on foot through many countries, begging our bread. At last we came to Sutri, tired and footsore and unable to go any farther. And, when none would take us in we found shelter in this cave to serve as a home until we could soften the anger of Charlemagne and obtain his forgiveness. But soon after you were born, Roland, the Pagan folk crossed the sea and threatened Rome. Then your father, remembering his knightly vows, once more donned his armor; and, taking his lance and his shield, went out to do battle for the king and the church. You know the rest, how he fought bravely and died. All this I have told you often. And now you have learned the story of your birth and your kinship. The blood that flows in your veins is the blood of heroes. You have seen Charlemagne, and today is the turning point in your life. Before the king leaves Sutri he must acknowledge you as his nephew and take you as a page into his court."

Young Roland – Part 1

Name: _____

I. Vocabulary: Underline the following words in the legend. Define each word and use it in a short sentence below.

○ garrison: _____

○ flaxen: _____

○ vanguard: _____

○ palfreys: _____

○ donned: _____

II. Plot: Write a simple sentence or phrase to describe the main actions that take place in each scene.

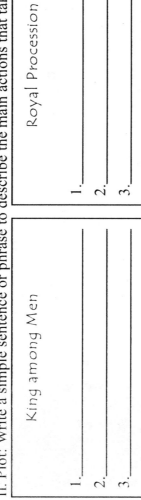

King among Men

1. _____

2. _____

3. _____

Royal Procession

1. _____

2. _____

3. _____

My Kinsfolk & Myself

1. _____

2. _____

3. _____

III. Characters: List and briefly describe the main characters in this legend.

_____

_____

_____

_____

IV. Rewrite this legend. Be sure to:

○ Include and underline all of the vocabulary words.

○ Write at least three separate paragraphs.

○ Include the following additional requirements.

Young Roland - Part 2

I

It was a great day in Sutri. Never since the old Roman days had so brilliant a company of warriors and noble men been seen in that quiet town. In the broad feast hall, Charlemagne and his peers were dining.

Mirth and revelry ruled the hour; and the long, low hall rang with the sound of the harp and the flute and the glad voices of the singers. The great oaken table groaned beneath its weight of good cheer. In the courtyard, around the open door, stood numbers of the poor people of the town, listening to the music, and waiting for the morsels that would be left after the feast. Suddenly a young boy, ragged and barefooted, appeared among them. All stood aside for him, as, with proud step and flashing eyes, he entered the great hall. With the air of a lord he pushed his way through the crowd of attendant knights and squires and walked boldly up to the table. Then, without saying a word, he seized upon a basket of rare fruit and a loaf of bread that had been placed before the king.

"Indeed," said Charlemagne, "that is a bold boy. He will make a brave knight."

But those who stood around were so awed by the lad's proud bearing and by the strange flash of his eyes that they dared not touch him; nor did they think of placing any hindrance in his way until he had seized the golden wine-cup which Charlemagne was on the point of lifting to his lips.

"Stop!" cried the king. "How dare you be so rude!"

But Roland held fast to his prize; and, fearless as a young eagle, he gazed into the face of the king. Charlemagne tried hard to appear angry; but, in spite of himself, a pleasant smile played upon his face, and his eyes twinkled merrily.

"My boy," said he, "the forest is a fitter place than this banquet hall for such as you. You would do better picking nuts from the trees than snatching dishes from the king's table; and the wine which you have taken from my hand is not nearly so good for you as the water in the flowing brook."

"The peasant drinks from the brook," answered Roland proudly; "the slave gathers nuts in the forest. But to my mother belong the best things that your table affords. The choicest game, the rarest fish, the reddest wine are hers."

"Ha!" cried the king. "Your mother must indeed be a noble lady! And I suppose you will tell me that she lives in a lordly castle. How many servants has she? Who is her carver? And who is her cup-bearer? Come, tell us all about it."

"My right hand is her carver," answered Roland, "and my left hand is her cup-bearer."

"And has she soldiers and watchmen, this wonderful mother of yours?"

"Indeed she has. These two arms are her soldiers and these eyes are her watchmen."

"That is a numerous household and a worthy one," answered the king, now very much amused. "But your good mother has strange taste in the matter of livery for her servants. I see they are all bareheaded and barefooted; and their clothing, what there is of it, is made of many colors. How came she to furnish you with a robe so rich and rare?"

"My robe is of my own furnishing," answered Roland. "Eight boys in the village do me homage; and they pay me tribute in cloth. And now, my lord, since you have learned all about my mother and her household, will you not visit her in her castle?"

Before the king could answer, the boy had turned on his heel, and, with the basket of food and the cup of wine in his hands, he fearlessly walked out of the hall. Charlemagne was surprised at the boldness of the lad and delighted with his witty answers.

II

"Let him go," said he. "A braver lad I have never seen; and he well deserves his prize. He will yet become the noblest knight in Christendom."

Then, turning to Duke Namon, he whispered, "Saw you that strange flash in his eye? Was there ever a fairer countenance or a more king-like form? Tell me truly, did he not remind you of someone you have seen elsewhere?"

"He did, my lord," answered Namon. "He reminded me of your worthy father, the great Pepin. He has the same noble features, the same broad brow, the same gray eyes flashing with a strange light. But he reminded me most of your lost sister. The same proud carriage of the head, the same curl of the lip, qualities that we once admired so much in the Lady Bertha, may all be seen in this wonderful boy."

Charlemagne at once ordered a dozen squires to follow the boy secretly to find where he dwelt and then, without harming him, to bring both him and his mother to the castle.

Very anxiously did the fair Bertha in the lonely hermit cell await the return of her son that day. He had left her in the morning, determined to make himself known to Charlemagne. He had promised to be back very soon. But hour after hour had passed by and still the boy did not come. Could it be possible that he had been too rash and had been imprisoned for his boldness? Bertha was about to despair of his return when Roland suddenly appeared around the foot of the hill, carrying on his left arm a basket of food and in his right hand a golden goblet of wine.

"Mother," he cried, as he set his burden down, "mother, I have brought you some share of the feast. You shall not starve while your brother eats and drinks so finely."

Then he placed all before her and, while she ate, he told her all that had happened to him. He had waited a long time about the palace doors, trying in vain to be allowed to see the king. At length, by the merest chance, he had peeped in through the open door of the banquet hall and had seen the king himself seated at the table.

"I could not bear," he said, "to see so great plenty of all that was good and know that you were here in this wretched cave without a morsel of food. I walked right in and took the best, nor did I regard that I was robbing the king. He talked to me and seemed not a bit angry; and I feel sure that he will send for me to come again before him, and then I will tell him all."

He had scarcely spoken these words, when the squires who had been sent in search of him came around the foot of the hill and halted only a few yards from the entrance to the grotto. Some were on foot, some on horseback; and all were armed with sticks. As soon as they saw Roland, they called out loudly to him, ordering him to surrender himself as their prisoner.

"Tell the king," he answered, "that I am holding high court at home today and that if he wants me, he must come after me himself."

"But you must come with us," cried the squires. "You and your mother the beggar woman must come with us and lose no time."

"Beggar woman, indeed!" cried Roland, overflowing with rage. "How dare you speak thus of the sister of Charlemagne? Go back to the king and tell him that his nephew is not wont to do the bidding of squires and churls. Tell him that only by the worthiest of his peers will my mother and I be taken into his presence."

At this the squires closed in upon him but Roland held them away with a stout club. It is uncertain how long this would have continued had the scene not been interrupted. A knight rode suddenly around the hill and reined up in the midst of the excited crowd.

III

"Ha, my brave men!" he cried in tones of merriment. "What have we here? What does it all mean?"

"It means," answered Roland, "that these want to take me by force to the king. Were they knights, or even gentlemen, I would go; but they are neither."

The knight was amused at the boy's earnestness; and he said, "I cannot blame you for refusing to be taken by them. Yet I know that the king wishes very much to see you and your mother, and he has sent me to hasten your coming. I am Namon, Duke of Bavaria, and I am sometimes known as one of Charlemagne's peers. Perhaps you will be willing to go with me if I send these squires away."

Roland, without a word of dissent, dropped his club to the ground and promised to go with the good knight at once if he would only find some means by which his mother might be helped to reach the castle without the fatigue of walking so far. Duke Namon dismounted from his steed and toward evening the noble duke, with Lady Bertha mounted behind him on a pillion and Roland following on foot, arrived in Sutri. Glad indeed was the greeting with which the king welcomed his sister; but not a word could the fair Bertha speak, so overwhelmed was she with gratitude.

"Sister," said the king, "for this boy's sake, if for nought else, all shall be forgiven. Let the past be forgotten in the joy of the present hour."

"Dear brother," said fair Bertha, "your kindness shall not go unrewarded. Roland will not disappoint you. He will grow up to be, next to you, the pattern of all heroes and the type of all manly virtues."

Indeed it happened so. Roland was trained as a squire under Duke Namon and became one of the twelve Peers of Charlemagne and a mighty hero.

Young Roland – Part 2

Name: _____

I. Vocabulary: Underline the following words in the legend. Define each word and use it in a short sentence below.

○ peers: _____

○ revelry: _____

○ amused: _____

○ livery: _____

○ grotto: _____

II. Plot: Write a simple sentence or phrase to describe the main actions that take place in each scene.

A Feast Interrupted	The Grotto	Sister Returns
1. _____	1. _____	1. _____
2. _____	2. _____	2. _____
3. _____	3. _____	3. _____

III. Characters: List and briefly describe the main characters in this legend.

_____

_____

_____

IV. Rewrite this legend. Be sure to:

○ Include and underline all of the vocabulary words.

○ Write at least three separate paragraphs.

○ Include the following additional requirements.

19

A Roland for an Oliver

I

Charlemagne held high festival at Paris in thanksgiving for the victories with which his armies had everywhere been blessed. Once more the foes of Christendom had been driven from Christian soil and the king had summoned the worthiest barons and warriors of his realm to award each some fitting recompense for his services. Among the knights who had come to Paris was old Count Gerard, the grandfather of Oliver and one of the most powerful barons of France. He had come to renew his homage for the ancient fief of Viana; and he hoped that the king, as a reward for his lifelong services, would grant him now the vacant fief of Burgundy. But, for some reason best known to himself, Charlemagne failed to invest him with the wished for dukedom.

After this Count Gerard rebelled against the king and declared that, for the affront which Charlemagne had offered him, he would no longer be his man nor pay him tribute. He shut himself up in the stronghold of Viana, which he victualed and strengthened with great care, and made ready for a long and close siege. He sent also to his brother Miles of Apulia and to his son Rainier of Genoa, craving their help. Miles came with a thousand men bearing shields and Rainier with two thousand crossbow-men. With Rainier came also his son Oliver, boldest of warriors, and his daughter Alda, beautiful as a Persian peri, brave as a Saxon valkyrie.

II

Great indeed was the siege which Charlemagne placed around Viana: none ever saw the like before. And he vowed that he would never leave it, nor give up the contest, until the proud Gerard should be humbled in the dust before him. For nine weeks he besieged the stronghold and allowed no one to come in or to go out; and yet so well supplied was the garrison with all things needful for life and comfort that they cared but little for the blockade. Neither besiegers nor besieged spared any pains to annoy one another. If Charlemagne's warriors dared approach too near the walls, they were driven back by a shower of arrows from the crossbows of the sharp-sighted Genoans. If the men of Viana ventured outside of the gates, a troop of fleet horsemen drove them back at the point of the lance. Day after day went by, the summer passed, and autumn came, and the war seemed no nearer at an end.

Some say that Charlemagne was encamped around Viana for seven years, but I think it could not have been more than seven months. Nevertheless, the whole country, for leagues on every side, was laid waste; and what had once been a blooming garden was now in a fair way to become a desert. The vineyards had been destroyed; the orchards had been cut down; the houses of the country folk had been burned and destroyed. Great, indeed, was the distress caused by this quarrel between the king and the count.

One day a party of strange knights rode into the camp of Charlemagne and asked to see the king without delay. They came from the mountain land which borders France on the south; and they brought stirring news, news which aroused the zeal of every loyal Christian warrior. Marsilius, the Pagan king of Spain, they said, had crossed the Pyrenees with a great host of Saracens and was carrying fire and sword and dire distress into the fairest provinces of Southern France. Unless Charlemagne should come quickly to the help of his people the Pagans would possess the richest portion of his kingdom.

The king was much troubled when he heard these tidings, and he called his peers together to ask their advice. All declared at once in favor of raising the siege of Viana, of making some sort of peace with Gerard, and marching without delay against the invaders. But Charlemagne remembered that before undertaking the siege of Viana, he had vowed not to desist until Count Gerard was humbled in the dust at his feet.

"I have an oath in heaven," said he, "and I must not break it. This traitor Gerard shall not be spared."

"Which were better," asked Duke Ganelon mildly, "to get a vow which was made too hastily or to sit here helpless and see all Christendom trodden under the feet of accursed Saracens?"

"It seems to me," said sage Duke Namon, "that the present business might be speedily ended by leaving it to the judgment of God. Count Gerard knows nothing of the straits that you are in: he cannot have heard of this invasion by the Saracens; and he will gladly agree to any arrangement that will bring our quarrel with him to an honorable end. Let two knights be chosen by lot, one from each party, and let the combat between them decide the question between you and Count Gerard."

Charlemagne and his peers were much pleased with this plan, and a messenger with a truce flag was sent into the fortress to propose the same to Count Gerard. The men of Viana were not only heartily tired of fighting against the king, but they foresaw that, if the siege were kept up much longer, they would be obliged to surrender for want of food; for their provisions were already beginning to run low. So they very gladly agreed to leave the whole matter to the decision of Heaven; and, as they numbered among them some of the bravest and most skillful swordsmen in Christendom, they had little doubt but that the judgment would be in their favor.

When the messenger came back to Charlemagne with count Gerard's answer, the king and his peers at once drew lots in order to determine which one of their number should be their champion. The lot fell upon Roland, and to him was assigned the danger and honor of maintaining the dignity and authority of the king and of deciding a question which many months of warfare and siege had failed to settle.

III

Early the following morning Roland was ferried over to an island meadow in the Rhone, where the knight who had been chosen by the Vianese folk to oppose him was already waiting. It was a knight with a red plume. Roland was well armed; but instead of his own shield he carried another, which the king had given; yet his good sword, Durandal the terror, slept in its sheath by his side, and with it alone he would have felt sure of victory. The Knight of the Red Plume had armed himself with the greatest care. His war coat had been wrought by the famed smith, the good Jew Joachim. The hauberk which he wore was the one which King Aeneas, ages before, had won from the Greeks on the plains of Troy. His buckler was of fishskin from the great salt sea, stretched on a frame of iron and hard enough to turn the edge of any common sword.

On one bank of the river stood the friends of Roland, anxious to see how the young hero would acquit himself, and yet not at all fearful of the result. On the other side were Count Gerard and the bravest knights and the fairest ladies of Viana.

The signal for the onset was given. The two knights put spurs to their steeds and dashed toward each other with the fury of tigers and the speed of the wind. The lances of both were shivered in pieces against the opposing shields, but neither was moved from his place in his saddle. Quickly, then, they dismounted and drew their swords.

Never before had there been so equal a fight. For more than two hours the two knights would thrust and parry, ward and strike; but neither gained the better of the other. At last, however, the sword of the red-plumed knight was broken by a too hasty blow upon Roland's helmet: his shield, too, was split from top to bottom. He had neither wherewith to fight nor to defend himself, yet he had made up his mind to die rather than to be vanquished, and he stood ready to fight with his fists. Roland was pleased to see such pluck, and he scorned to take advantage of his foe's ill plight.

"Friend," said he right courteously, "full great is your pride, and I love you for it. You have lost your sword and your shield, while my good Durandal has neither notch nor blemish. Nephew am I to the king of France. Great shame would be upon me were I to slay an unarmed man when he is in my power. Chose you now another sword and a more trusty shield and meet me again as my equal."

Roland sat down upon the grass and rested himself, while the red-plumed knight bade his squires bring him another sword from the castle. Soon both parties were armed and the fierce fight began again. Never were weapons wielded with greater skill; never was there a nobler combat. The sun rose high in the heavens, and still each knight stood firmly in his place, gaining no vantage over his foe. After a time, however, the patience of the red-plumed knight gave out. He grew furious. He struck savagely at Roland; but the stroke was skillfully warded, and the red-plumed knight's sword broke near the handle. At the same time Durandal, coming down with the force of a thunderbolt, buried itself so deeply in the shield of the red-plumed knight that Roland could not withdraw it.

Both knights were thus made weaponless, but neither was vanquished. Wrathfully they rushed together to seize each other and to throw the other down. Moved by the same thought each snatched the other's helmet and lifted it from his head. As they stood there, bareheaded and face to face, memories of their boyhood came back to them. Both were struck dumb with astonishment for a moment. Roland saw before him his loved brother-in-arms, Oliver. Oliver, now no longer the red-plumed knight, recognized his old friend Roland. Then they rushed into each other's arms.

"I am conquered!" cried Roland.

"I yield me!" cried Oliver.

The people on the shore knew not what to make of all this. Presently they saw the two late antagonists standing hand in hand, and it was evident the battle was at an end. The knights crowded round them, and with one voice hailed them as equals in glory. If there were any who felt disposed to murmur that the battle was left undecided, they were silenced by the voice of Ogier the Dane, who proclaimed aloud that all had been done that honor required and declared that he would maintain that award against all gainsayers.

The quarrel with Gerard being left undecided, a truce was made for four days, and in that time, by the efforts of Duke Namon on the one side and of Oliver on the other, a reconciliation was effected. Charlemagne, accompanied by Gerard, marched to meet Marsilius, who hastened to retreat across the frontier.

A Roland for an Oliver

Name: _____

I. Vocabulary: Underline the following words in the legend. Define each word and use it in a short sentence below.

○ homage: _____

○ fief: _____

○ obliged: _____

○ hauberk: _____

○ antagonists: _____

II. Plot: Write a simple sentence or phrase to describe the main actions that take place in each scene.

Paris Thanksgiving

1. _____
2. _____
3. _____

Siege

1. _____
2. _____
3. _____

I am Conquered

1. _____
2. _____
3. _____

III. Characters: List and briefly describe the main characters in this legend.

_____

_____

_____

IV. Rewrite this legend. Be sure to:

○ Include and underline all of the vocabulary words.

○ Write at least three separate paragraphs.

○ Include the following additional requirements.

The Death of Roland - Part 1

Charlemagne had made war in Spain for nigh seven years, and he had conquered almost the whole of that fair country; for there remained only the city of Saragossa over which King Marsilas still reigned.

As Charlemagne sat upon a fair throne in a spacious orchard, there came to him ten ambassadors from Saragossa, bringing word from that same King Marsilas. The ambassadors rode upon white mules that were bedecked with much richness, they carried olive branches in their hands, and their bearing was courteous.

When these men had approached near to the Emperor, they made due reverence and said: "Sire, we are come as ambassadors from King Marsilas. The message that King Marsilas hath put into our lips is this message: that he wearies him of so much warfare and perceives right well the valor of the noble knights of France and it seems to him that the faith which is held by thee is a true faith. For these reasons his prayer is that thou wilt have pity on him. And if thou wilt leave this Kingdom of Spain to him and wilt return to thine own country of France, he makes fair promise that he will follow thee thither within a month's time and will be baptized into thy faith; and he will do thee homage, as thy vassal, for the Kingdom of Spain."

The Emperor sank his beard upon his breast and thought long upon this speech, and when he had reflected, he said: "The King hath long been mine enemy, how shall I know that he means well by me?"

The ambassadors replied: "He will send thee hostages, as many as thou wilt; for it is a true word that he is tired of warfare and would fain see this strife ended."

Said Charlemagne: "On the morrow we will speak again upon this matter; and if it be as ye have said, then shall my heart be glad."

II

So the Emperor ordered that provision should be made for the ambassadors, and when the morrow was come, he called his nobles together; and he related to them all the messengers had said.

Now Roland, who was nephew to the Emperor and the knight feared most of all by the heathen, believed that King Marsilas harbored treachery in his heart and that the message held false promises, and he recalled to the Emperor how King Marsilas had deceived him in days gone by and how he was a man of a crafty and ungenerous spirit.

But after Roland had spoken, there spake Ganelon, he who would have been a most perfect knight had his word been as true as his body was fair; but he was a man of a weak character who could be won over to evil things.

Ganelon said: "Sire, I see no reason to doubt the intention of King Marsilas. Is it not a true thing which he saith: that there hath been warfare enough to weary a man? Now I say it were unseemly in a Christian King to reject the advances of a heathen when he would accept the true faith. For what, sire, have we conquered Spain, if not to bring glory to the Cross?"

When these words were spoken, they seemed to Charlemagne wise words and generous counsel; and he turned to that wise and venerable noble, the Duke of Bavaria, and said: "What thinkest thou of these counsels which have been given to me by Roland and by Ganelon?"

The Duke replied for albeit he was cautious, he was mellow with years, "I think with Ganelon that it were ill to refuse this offer of King Marsilas. Yet I would ask for hostages."

Charlemagne said, "It is good; we shall act on the advice. Therefore I shall send a knight to treat with this King and to bear to him a letter. Now which of ye shall go?"

Then proffered Roland and Oliver and the Duke of Bavaria and many another. But the Emperor had good reasons why none of these should go. And, being weary with discussion of the matter, he said to the nobles: "Ye shall agree among yourselves who shall go."

And after some discussion Roland said that Ganelon should go; nor had he any ill-will toward Ganelon in suggesting this thing, since he would himself have gone gladly; and the other knights agreed.

But Ganelon, when he had given his counsel to the Emperor, had not thought of himself as messenger in the matter and he believed that Roland spake in hatred when he proposed that Ganelon should go. Therefore he looked upon Roland with a glance that was evil; and all knights saw that Ganelon was ill-pleased to go.

When Ganelon was ready to set forth, having received advice from his Emperor, he looked again upon Roland before he went; and in a low voice he said, "Have a care, Count Roland; where Ganelon loses a feather he claims a wing. And it may be that thou shalt hear again of this matter."

Roland replied, "I have worked thee no ill, Ganelon, therefore I fear nothing."

And Ganelon set out. When he had journeyed some little distance, he came up with the ambassadors of King Marsilas, who had started a little while before him to return to their king.

On the way these men conversed with Ganelon, and having treated him very pleasantly, they begged of him that he would tell them if the Emperor thought kindly of the petition of their king.

Then spake Ganelon, "Charlemagne is as strong now as he hath ever been, and his years sit lightly upon him. Nevertheless, but for Roland, he would content him with less warfare. Roland it is ever, that proud peer, who inciteth him to the taking of new cities." And Ganelon spoke other such things to arouse the anger of the ambassadors toward Roland.

Then the ambassadors said angrily, "We like not this Roland, tell us how Charlemagne may be rid of him, and we will give thee great treasure, we and our lord."

And Ganelon, though at first he felt anger at this speech and told himself he would work no evil against any brother-knight, afterwards consented to talk with the ambassadors about a means to compass Roland's downfall; for he felt his hate surge within him.

III

Then Ganelon came before King Marsilas, and, having saluted him with all courtesy, he related that message which he carried. And he related it with truth, for the hate which he bore to Roland he bore only to Roland; to Charlemagne he was a faithful knight, where Roland was not concerned.

Said Ganelon, standing straight and still, "This is the message of my lord, the great Charlemagne: that he is well pleased that ye desire baptism into the true faith, all ye of Saragossa, for so ye shall save your souls. As for Spain, he will yield to thee one-half of it, to hold as vassal; for the other half is for Count Roland. In one month's time ye shall follow him to France and be baptized, as hath been promised. But if ye follow not, then he will lay siege to Saragossa and take the city; and thou and thy knights shall be degraded and shall be carried away."

King Marsilas was so filled with anger at this speech, that, rising from his throne, he would have killed Ganelon had not his chiefs restrained him. Then the ambassadors, having gained the ear of the King, declared to him how Ganelon would aid him in bringing about the downfall of that great knight Roland and perchance of Oliver and of others of the Twelve Peers of France.

"When Charlemagne hath been so maimed in his power and his affection, he will no longer incline toward warfare, and our country shall be left to us in peace," they said; and at these words King Marsilas looked again upon Ganelon, and he perceived that he was a brave man on occasion but weak through his passions and that his hatred of Roland would make him traitor so that he would serve them.

Therefore, coming again to Ganelon, he treated him softly and told him how he thought well of the message of his lord and asked him how they should be rid of Roland.

Said Ganelon, "In all things I shall be true to Charlemagne; but as for Roland, my soul hates him. Now this is my advice to ye, that ye send to the Emperor the hostages he demands, and ye shall treat him fairly, and with a good heart; and ye shall declare to him how, if he hasten to France, ye will follow him in a short period. Now when Charlemagne goes he will leave some behind to guard the passes; and I promise ye that in the rearguard there shall be Roland and Oliver and others of the Peers of France.

"They will have but twenty thousand men, and the number of ye all is four hundred thousand men. Therefore ye shall come upon Roland, having parted your hosts, in divisions, fighting with him one, two, or maybe three or four battles. Thus will his strength be wrested from him, and he shall be in your hands.

"But if ye fall upon him in the pride of your full numbers, then will Roland blow a blast from that horn of his; and there will come Charlemagne, hastening back from that place where he may be; and ye shall suffer a great defeat. And Roland's fame shall be increased to your dismay."

When King Marsilas and his chiefs heard these words, they were filled with admiration of the wisdom of Ganelon and with joy at that which he proposed. And having loaded him with gifts for his Emperor, they allowed him to depart.

And Ganelon went away with joy and shame writ large upon his face.

The Death of Roland – Part 1

Name: _____

I. Vocabulary: Underline the following words in the legend. Define each word and use it in a short sentence below.

○ bedecked: _____

○ homage: _____

○ vassal: _____

○ siege: _____

○ traitor: _____

II. Plot: Write a simple sentence or phrase to describe the main actions that take place in each scene.

Proposal from the King	Charlemagne's Answer	Traitorous Plots
1. _____	1. _____	1. _____
2. _____	2. _____	2. _____
3. _____	3. _____	3. _____

III. Characters: List and briefly describe the main characters in this legend.

_____

_____

_____

IV. Rewrite this legend. Be sure to:

○ Include and underline all of the vocabulary words.

○ Write at least three separate paragraphs.

○ Include the following additional requirements.

The Death of Roland - Part 2

I

Then Ganelon approached Charlemagne, and he delivered to his lord the message of King Marsilas, that the King agreed to all that had been proposed. And Charlemagne said, "I take great pleasure in these things, for I would have Spain governed by Christian lords. To God be the glory!"

And he arranged that he would move on toward France without further delay.

Then came up the matter of the rear-guard which should remain to guard these narrow passes. Ganelon said, "Sire, it would be well done to leave Roland, thy nephew, that valiant knight, for of his very name those heathen have a fear."

Charlemagne said, "The advice sounds good to me. What sayest thou, Roland?"

And Roland suspected Ganelon but he replied, "Sire, I wish for naught better than to guard these passes for thee. And I thank Ganelon for his praise."

Then Ganelon changed color, and he would not look at Roland.

And there remained with Roland Oliver his comrade and the Archbishop Turpin, a man of great wit and much valour, and in all the Twelve Peers of France. And Charlemagne made offer to Roland of a great army of soldiers, but he would have no more than twenty thousand.

When all these things were arranged, Charlemagne departed through the valley of Roncesvalles; and the noise of his army's passing grew fainter and fainter until it died.

Now that sound was not long dead when Roland heard another sound upon the air. First it was feeble and soft, like the hum of insects, then it was stronger and louder, like the ring of horses' hoofs; and afterwards it was a great noise.

Then said Oliver to Roland: "Lo, the drums! The Saracens are upon us. Now I understand that look on the face of Ganelon! Rest assured, he has sold us to the enemy."

Roland mounted upon a hill; and when he had stood there for a while, he returned and said: "The enemy are indeed upon us, and I have never seen the like, for in number they are as the sands of the sea."

Then Oliver also mounted to the hill-top, and when he had returned, he said to Roland, "Count Roland, set thy horn to thy lips and blow; for the heathen are passing many, and we are but a few; and it were well that Charlemagne should hear thy blast and should return and should help us. For we know not the end of the mischief which Ganelon hath brought upon us."

"Nay," said Roland, "I shall not yet sound my horn. Hath not Charlemagne set us here to do service for him, and we have done nothing? Not till I am sore pressed will I sound my horn. As for Ganelon, blame him not, for we know not that he had a hand in this."

Oliver was sore troubled, for it lay upon his soul that the close of this day would bring great grief to the heart of France. And again he besought Roland to sound his horn. But Roland would not.

Now the men of France were drawn up in array upon the plain and they beheld the heathen who were close upon them and the numbers of the heathen were at least one hundred thousand men.

Roland saw that it would be a hard battle, but he didn't know that these were but a quarter of the men whom King Marsilas and his chiefs held ready for battle, else had he not refused to sound his ivory horn.

Then Roland called upon the knights that they should wage war with a good will and bring honor to Charlemagne; and he said how he knew not what treachery had worked this evil but that it might be brought to a good issue, by God's grace, if they all worked together with a good heart.

Then that brave Archbishop Turpin gave them absolution from their sins, every man; and having prayed to God, they awaited the onslaught of the heathen. And the heathen advanced, taunting the knights of France, telling them how they had been betrayed and had been left now by Charlemagne to die and how France would that day lose her fair fame.

II

Roland replied naught in words. But as the armies came together Roland laid about him with great blows, such blows as had made him famous, and Oliver fought with a fury as great, and the other Peers also fought with valor; and against these rode out the knights of King Marsilas, who came on, each one with bold words and looks, and thrust themselves upon the French with a mighty force.

And as each came forward, he was laid upon the field, so great was the valor of Roland and of Oliver and of others beside.

Still the heathen came on, and their numbers were so great that they appeared to have no end. They fought passing well, those Peers of France! Yet were they sore beset because of the numbers of the heathen.

King Almiras was one of those who held a division for King Marsilas. He wound with his men through an unknown pass and found the rear of the Frenchmen and fell upon them there.

26

And when the Peers of France beheld them, they were disturbed, for they were as a rushing flood, without end or limit. And the men of France thought of Ganelon with hatred and with bitter reproach. But the Archbishop called to them that they should think not of Ganelon's treachery but of France and their own duty and how to die as brave men.

Thus were they minded of their duty, and they spoke no more of Ganelon; but instead held themselves ready to do great deeds.

And they said, "Charlemagne shall suffer no shame through our work this day. We shall die as brave men, having taken our toll of the heathen."

Now they encountered the heathen, and the shock of the encounter was as the meeting of great waters; for there was no man who would shrink back, nay, not one.

Yet the heathen came on again a fourth and a fifth time; and they were beaten back. Now the last time they were so beaten there remained of the Frenchmen less than one hundred.

Then was Roland sad almost to tears, looking upon what was left of the men of France; and he reproached himself in his heart that he had not, as Oliver had advised him, blown a blast upon his horn. For he had not fathomed Ganelon's treachery.

That time was over, and Charlemagne might not arrive now soon enough to help them. Nevertheless, that he might learn of their plight and might avenge them, Roland raised his horn to his lips and blew a blast that shook the air.

III

Now Charlemagne heard the sound, as it were an echo that faintly troubled the stillness. And he said, "It is the horn of Roland. Some evil hath come to him."

"Sire," said Ganelon, "what evil should come to Roland? Of a surety nothing evil hath befallen him. Thy thoughts are with him, and thy fancy plays on thee."

And the Emperor was silent, for he was not sure what he had heard.

But Roland blew again, a sharp shrill blast that cut the air and reached to the ear of the Emperor.

"Now," said he, "Roland surely calls. What hath befallen him I know not, but I know right well that he hath need of me." And he bade that they should return.

Now they had but turned them about, when Roland raised his horn to his lips for the third time; and he blew a call that went winding through the passes, full of sorrow and grief and farewell. Said the Emperor, "There hath been treachery. Roland is nigh to death. Now if I lose him I lose half my life." And he went threading back the way he had come and with him his hosts.

Now the enemy was again upon that brave Roland and the remnant of the men of France and fell upon the men of France, and they wounded Oliver so that he might not live. But Oliver, ere the breath went from his lips, called to Roland, he bade him farewell. And soon after Oliver died.

Then were there left of the men of France but three, Roland, Walter, and that Archbishop whom they loved. And these three fought fiercely against the enemy, waking in them such great fear that they durst not advance closely but threw spears and javelins and other weapons.

In this fashion was slain Walter, and the Archbishop was wounded near to death. And Roland stood alone, fighting most furiously; and such havoc did he alone, and with his horse killed under him, that the heathen fled from him and left him there.

Then Roland went into the field, seeking the bodies of those he loved; and when he had found the Peers of France, he bore them with an exceeding tenderness to the Archbishop where he lay dying and set them before him.

Now the Archbishop gave his last blessing, and when he had given it he died, laying his head upon the grass.

And Roland felt upon himself a great faintness, and he knew that his life was nearly done. Then he made his way to a little hill where there were marble steps; and upon these steps he tried to break his sword before he died; but he could not break it.

Then he set his horn and his sword upon the hillside and lay upon them so that they were hidden. And he prayed to God to forgive all his sins.

And when he had prayed this prayer a second time, he rested his head upon his arm and died.

The Death of Roland – Part 2

Name: _____

I. Vocabulary: Underline the following words in the legend. Define each word and use it in a short sentence below.

○ Twelve Peers of France: _____

○ sound: _____

○ heathen: _____

○ absolution: _____

○ valor: _____

II. Plot: Write a simple sentence or phrase to describe the main actions that take place in each scene.

Lo, the Drums!	Bold Words and Looks	Three Blasts
1. _____	1. _____	1. _____
2. _____	2. _____	2. _____
3. _____	3. _____	3. _____

III. Characters: List and briefly describe the main characters in this legend.

_____

_____

_____

IV. Rewrite this legend. Be sure to:

○ Include and underline all of the vocabulary words.

○ Write at least three separate paragraphs.

○ Include the following additional requirements.

How Oliver Fought for France and the Faith

I

The French camp lay as still as a hive of drowsy bees. Perhaps the stillness was the one sign of the great battle and victory of a few days since. It told of weary warriors within the tents; it told also of brave knights grievously wounded; it told of the peace that treads close upon the heels of victory.

But that peace was rudely broken. Suddenly upon the air came a heavy sound as of the thunder of horses' hoofs. It came nearer and nearer. Then there came into view, breaking the peace of the place, a horseman in armor, a horseman so immense that he seemed to fill the horizon and dominate the plain. He rode upon a horse as great as he and flashed across the plain like a lightning of sunlight, drawing rein at last before the royal tent of Charlemagne.

There he halted and upraised his voice, which was like the roar of some angry creature other than man. "Behold, great Charlemagne," said he, "I have sought thy camp and would honor thy knights by doing battle with them. Send out Roland or Oliver or another of like prowess, that by showing him his littleness I may take pleasure in mine own strength. Nay, send out Roland and Oliver and another with them; send out seven knights if thou wilt. Have not I in my time slain kings, and is not my strength equal to that of ten men?"

This furious roar came to the ears of Charlemagne, and he halted in his speech to his knights. "Tell me," said he to one of the dukes, "who is this champion whose mouth is so full of words?"

The duke replied, "He is Fierabras the giant, son of Balan, an admiral of the Moors. By repute I know him well, and it is true that in his time he hath slain many valiant men and overcome kings. Moreover, he hath done many evil deeds among Christians, and it is he who hath in his possession the sacred tomb of our Lord."

The Emperor's brow grew dark as he heard these words. "My brave knights," said Charlemagne, lifting his glance from the ground, "which from among ye shall do battle with this braggart, for the defense of our faith and the fair fame of France?"

After this question there came a murmur, as of men who would fain speak yet would not suffer themselves; but after the murmur there came a silence, and the knights answered not a word. Then cast the Emperor a glance upon the company, but not yet with anger in it, for he was amazed and did not understand. Now the glance of the Emperor rested last upon Roland, who was his own nephew. And Roland, feeling the sting of the Emperor's wonder found his voice. "Sire," said he, "cast thine ear back to listen to thine own words. After that fight in which we, thy knights, fought valiantly, bringing to thee victory--and to Oliver, mine own friend, many wounds so that he is like to die--didst not thou make little honor of our valor? For you said that we, thy knights, had indeed fought bravely but that our deeds were as shadows compared with what the old knights had done in our place. Good Uncle, of all these old knights, surely one remaineth! Bid him that he do battle with Fierabras."

Then indeed bitterness rose to the Emperor's lips and would have overflowed had not the roar of the giant again burst forth, swallowing all lesser sounds. "Haste thee, Charlemagne," cried he, "and send forth one who shall do battle for thee! While I wait for him, I will refresh myself with sleep beneath yonder tree. But I swear to thee that, if thou send no one, then shall I come with my hosts, and when I have swung thy head in my hands, I will seize thy peers and degrade them, and I will wipe thine army out of this land."

When he had spoken these words, the giant wheeled about and rode furiously to a tree that grew upon the plain. Having reached it, he stripped himself of his armor and lay down as if he would sleep. Then Charlemagne, pale with his great anger and the insults that the giant had offered him, broke into speech against Roland, and the quarrel between them waxed great.

II

Fierabras the giant slept, but his challenge had carried far, reaching the ears of Oliver, Roland's friend, as he lay ill of his wounds. Therefore Oliver called his squire, Garin, and bade him to discover the meaning of the hubbub.

Garin was gone a long time. When he returned he related to Oliver how Fierabras had offered battle; and he told how no knight would offer to fight with him and of the quarrel between Roland and Charlemagne. Then Oliver was silent for a space, for he knew that his wounds worried Roland, making sorer the recollection of the Emperor's careless words. And as Garin waited, his breast full of shame, the voice of Oliver came, bidding him to bring him his armor and set it upon him. Garin brought the armor, and when Oliver had bathed his wounds and bound them, Garin put the armor upon him and Oliver mounted his horse and made his way to the tent of the Emperor.

When he had found it, he came before Charlemagne, who sat silent. And Charlemagne at first believed him to be a vision. Then perceiving that this was indeed his knight Oliver, he cried: "Sir Oliver, Sir Oliver, get thee back to thy bed! What folly is this? Wouldst thou call Death ere he have thought of thee?"

Oliver replied, heeding not the throbbing of his wounds, "Sire, I have found thee that I may crave of thee a favor. Since for many a year I have fought, asking nothing, I beg of thee to grant this, my request."

Now Charlemagne believed that Oliver had a fever upon him and understood not his own words. Therefore he answered him, "My good Oliver, thy favor is granted thee. Ask what thou wilt; there is naught among my possessions I would refuse you. But haste thee back to thy bed, that thy wounds may be quiet and grow whole."

Oliver replied in a voice that rang clear as a silver trumpet. "My request has nothing to do with possessions. It is, sire, that I be allowed to do battle with this heathen. When I have done this thing I will take heed of my wounds."

Then the Emperor slid his head upon his hands and was troubled; for he had granted Oliver his request, not knowing the purport of it, and might not take back his royal word; yet he was assured that Oliver had no strength with which to fight Fierabras and that he would speedily die through the severity of his wounds.

"Nay, Oliver," said he, "rest and grow whole. A wounded knight cannot fight the giant."

But Oliver replied firmly, "It is my request, which has been granted to me. Therefore, sire, let me go."

And while the knights about the Emperor grew pale with many emotions, Oliver took from Charlemagne his glove that he might bear it with him to the fight. And when he had found Fierabras, he cried to him, "Awake, Fierabras, the great Charlemagne hath sped me forth to do battle with thee."

And at the cry the giant bestirred himself and when he perceived Oliver, he rose to his feet.

Then said Oliver, "This is the message of that great and Christian Emperor who hath sent me: 'Thou shalt forsake thine idols and worship the one true God. '"

But Fierabras replied, "I will not."

Then spake Oliver, "Wilt thou leave this land, that we may make it Christian?"

Then replied Fierabras, rearing his head and speaking proudly, "I am Fierabras, a heathen prince and of great power. I have done evil to many Christians. These messages which thou bearest to me are but idle words which I heed as lightly as I heed the wind that blows, for I hold in contempt thy country and thy faith."

Then was Oliver shaken with anger so that his wounds bled; and in a voice that was quiet because of his anger he answered, "Since thou hast spurned the alternative offered, haste thee and fight with me, for I am eager to begin."

"Help me, then," said Fierabras, "to put on mine armor, for it is of great weight." And Oliver helped him, fearing nothing; neither did the giant do him any ill.

III

Therefore they betook them to a fair place on the plain in which to do battle, and from the French hosts came out many to watch the fight. And when all was ready they flew together; and with such swiftness and force that their forms appeared but as quickly moving flashes of sunlight, and their spears in a trice were broken in twain.

Now, Fierabras had three famous swords, which he named Pleasaunce, Baptism, and Grabon. From these he chose Pleasaunce, that he might give to that sword the joy of overcoming so brave a knight. And, having gripped the sword, he flew again upon Oliver as if he would have cut him in pieces. But Oliver answered the thrust with one mightier and better placed, thus breaking off a part of the giant's helmet, which fell to the ground.

Said Charlemagne, under his breath, "God hath blessed us, and the fight is to our wounded Oliver."

The words had but stirred the air when Oliver's shield received a blow that brake it; and it seemed that the knight staggered from the force of the blow and from the weakness his wounds bred in him. Charlemagne drooped his head and prayed.

Yet Oliver recovered himself bravely, crushing his strength into a thrust that had almost finished the giant; and again the contest waxed fierce. Heavily breathed Fierabras as he fought, and Oliver, that valiant knight, while his wounds burnt his flesh, pressed close upon the giant, his eyes darting glances that were like flames.

"It is a valiant knight," thought Fierabras, and for the first time he questioned the issue of the fight; then with a new strength he fell hard upon Oliver, and to such good purpose, that he struck the knight's sword from his hand and sent it hurtling to the ground.

"Ah, Sir Oliver!" cried Fierabras, lifting up his voice in mockery. "Where is now the strength thy God hath promised thee and of what avail would it be to thee since thou mayest not recover thy sword?"

Oliver answered nothing, being hard put to it in his thoughts to discover a way out of his difficulty. For he would have sought his sword where it lay, covering himself with his shield meanwhile, had not the shield lain in pieces upon the ground. As for his armor, it was battered and broken upon him. And the pain of his wounds waxed intolerable.

By reason of his pain the knight turned pale, and Fierabras, when he perceived it, was filled with compassion for this brave knight, whom he liked not ill.

"See, Sir Oliver," said he, "I will wait while thou liftest thy sword."

"Nay," cried Oliver, "that would be no victory which I should owe to thy clemency!"

And even as he spoke, he prayed in his heart for strength and succor. Thereafter the prayer having left his lips, Oliver looked about him and immediately perceived the giant's second sword--Baptism--which lay behind him close to his hand; for in the heat of the fight they had neared the spot where the giant had placed his other swords.

"Behold, Fierabras," cried he, "by the aid of thine own sword shall I work thine undoing!" and he gripped the sword hardly and ran upon him with a mighty force.

Now Fierabras, whether by reason of his confusion and dismay on perceiving his own sword turned against him or by reason of his weariness, received the onslaught but ill, and having dealt Oliver a cut that miscarried, received one in his turn that caught him heavily, piercing his side, so that he fell with a crash upon the ground.

Oliver, seeing his adversary so defeated, durst not himself move, lest, since all his strength had gone into the blow he had given, he should fall for lack of it. Thus he bowed his head in humble gladness upon his breast, the while the French hosts rent the air with great cries of joy; and his thoughts wound into a prayer of thanksgiving to that Great God who had given to him the victory through the strength that He had bestowed.

Fierabras the giant recovered from his wound and was baptized into the true faith. For the evil he had done, he made generous recompense. Of the brave deeds he did thereafter, he made little boast. He became one of the twelve Peers of France and I trow there were few knights more valiant than he.

How Oliver Fought for France and the Faith

Name: _____

I. Vocabulary: Underline the following words in the legend. Define each word and use it in a short sentence below.

○ prowess: _____

○ braggart: _____

○ hubbub: _____

○ heathen: _____

○ clemency: _____

II. Plot: Write a simple sentence or phrase to describe the main actions that take place in each scene.

Mouth Full of Words	Throbbing Wounds	Generous Recompense
1. _____	1. _____	1. _____
2. _____	2. _____	2. _____
3. _____	3. _____	3. _____

III. Characters: List and briefly describe the main characters in this legend.

_____

_____

_____

IV. Rewrite this legend. Be sure to:

○ Include and underline all of the vocabulary words.

○ Write at least three separate paragraphs.

○ Include the following additional requirements.

31

Balmung and Greyfell

I

At Santen, in the Lowlands, there once lived a young prince named Siegfried. His father, Siegmund, was king of a rich country; and he was known, both far and near, for his good deeds. Siegfried's mother, the gentle Sigelind, was loved by all for her goodness of heart and her kindly charity to the poor. Neither king nor queen left aught undone that might make the young prince happy or fit him for life's usefulness. Wise men were brought from far-off lands to be his teachers; and every day something was added to his store of knowledge or his stock of happiness. And very skillful did he become in warlike games and in manly feats of strength. No other youth could throw the spear with such great force or shoot the arrow with surer aim. No other youth could run more swiftly or ride with more becoming ease. His gentle mother took delight in adding to the beauty of his matchless form by clothing him in costly garments decked with the rarest jewels. One would have thought that the life of the young prince could never be aught but a holiday and that the birds would sing and the sun would shine forever for his sake.

But the business of man's life is not mere pastime; and none knew this truth better than the wise old king, Siegmund.

"All work is noble," said he to Siegfried, "and he who yearns to win fame must not shun toil. Even princes should know how to earn a livelihood by the labor of their hands."

And so, while Siegfried was still a young lad, his father sent him to live with a smith called Mimer, whose smithy was among the hills not far from the great forest. And this smith Regin was a wonderful master, the wisest and most cunning that the world had ever seen. Men said that he was akin to the dwarf-folk who had ruled the earth in the early days; and they said that he was so exceeding old that no one could remember the day when he came to dwell in the land of Siegmund's fathers.

To Regin's school, where he would be taught to work skillfully and to think wisely, Siegfried was sent to be in all respects like the other pupils there. A coarse blue blouse and heavy leggings and a leathern apron took the place of the costly clothing which he had worn in his father's dwelling. The dainty bed, with its downy pillows, wherein every night his mother had seen him safely covered, was given up for a rude heap of straw in a corner of the smithy. And the rich food to which he had been used gave place to the coarsest and humblest fare. But the lad did not complain. The days which he passed in the smithy were mirthful and happy; and the sound of his hammer rang cheerfully, and the sparks from his forge flew briskly from morning till night.

And a wonderful smith he became. No one could do more work than he, and none wrought with greater skill. The heaviest chains and the strongest bolts were but as toys in his stout hands, so easily and quickly did he beat them into shape. And he was alike cunning in work of the most delicate and brittle kind. Ornaments of gold and silver, studded with the rarest jewels, were fashioned into beautiful forms by his deft fingers. And among all of Regin's apprentices none learned the master's lore so readily or gained the master's favor so quickly.

II

Now Siegfried longed to be like the heroes of old and he begged Regin to make him a sword that he might have a weapon to go into the world with and right wrongs.

So Regin, with his heart full of hope, went to his task. And for seven days and seven nights the sparks never stopped flying from his forge; and the ringing of his anvil and the hissing of the hot metal as he tempered it were heard continuously. On the eighth day the sword was finished, and he brought it to Siegfried who felt the razor edge of the bright weapon and said, "This seems, indeed, a fair edge. Let us make a trial its temper."

With that Siegfried raised the sword and brought it down with a mighty force upon the anvil where it shivered into a thousand pieces. So Regin went back to work and again made a sword and again Siegfried broke it upon the anvil. This happened again and again till one day Siegfried went home and told his mother how he could not find a sword strong enough for him to wield. Then with great care she brought to him a cloth bag and in it was a wondrous sword which was broken in two. "This," she explained, "was once your father's sword. Take it and forge it anew."

Then Siegfried went and welded the sword in a white-hot fire and tempered it with milk and oatmeal. For seven weeks the lad wrought day and night at his forge; and then, pale and haggard but with a pleased smile upon his face, he stood before Regin, with the gleaming sword in his hands. "It is finished," he said. "Behold the glittering terror! - the blade Balmung. Let us try its edge and prove its temper."

Siegfried raised the blade high over his head; and the gleaming edge flashed hither and thither, like the lightning's play when Thor rides over the storm clouds. Then suddenly it fell upon the master's anvil, and the great block of iron was cleft in two; but the bright blade was no whit dulled by the stroke and the line of light which marked the edge was brighter than before.

Then to the flowing brook they went; and a great pack of wool, the fleeces of ten sheep, was brought and thrown upon the swirling water. As the stream bore the bundle downwards, Regin held the sword in its way. And when the wool floated against the sword the bundle was divided cleanly in two.

III

"Well done!" cried the delighted smith. "Never have I seen a keener edge."

Then Siegfried begged of Regin "Tell me, wisest of masters, what shall I do to win fame and to make myself worthy to rule the fair land which my fathers held?"

Regin replied, "Go forth to right the wrong, to punish evil, and come not back until the world knows your noble deeds."

"But whither shall I go?" asked Siegfried.

"I will tell you," said Regin. "Gird about you this sword, the good Balmung, and go northward. When you come to the waste lands which border upon the sea, you will find the ancient Gripir, the last of the kin of the giants. Ask of him a war steed, and Odin will tell you the rest."

So, when the sun had risen, Siegfried bade Regin good-by and went forth like a man to take whatsoever fortune should betide. He went through the great forest and across the bleak moorlands beyond and over the huge black mountains and came to a pleasant country dotted with farmhouses and yellow with waving corn. But he tarried not here. Right onwards he went, until he reached the place where the high mountains stood, and there in the deep dales between the mountains were rich meadows, green with grass, where herds of cattle and deer and untamed horses fed in undisturbed peace. And Siegfried, when he saw, knew that these were the pastures of Gripir the ancient.

High among the gray mountain peaks stood Gripir's dwelling, a mighty house made of huge boulders brought by giant hands from the far northland. But Siegfried was not afraid. He climbed the steep pathway which the feet of men had never touched before and, without pausing, walked straightway into the high hall. There he saw beneath a heavy canopy of stone, the ancient Gripir. Very wise he seemed, and he gazed at Siefgried with a smile.

"Hail Siegfried!" he cried. "Welcome to my lonely mountain home! Come and sit by my side in the high-seat where man has never sat, and I will tell thee of things that have been and of things that are yet to be."

Then Siegfried fearlessly went and sat by the side of the ancient one. And long hours they talked together, strong youth and hoariest age; and each was glad that in the other he had found some source of hope and comfort. At last Gripir rose and said, "Thou hast not told me of thy errand, but I know what it is. Come with me and choose from my pastures a battle steed and ride forth to win a name and fame among the sons of men."

And Siegfried ran down the steep side of the mountain to the grassy dell where the horses were feeding. But the beasts were all so fair and strong, that he knew not which to choose. While he paused, uncertain what to do, a strange man stood before him. Tall and handsome was the man, with one bright eye, and a face beaming like the dawn in summer; and upon his head he wore a sky-blue hood bespangled with golden stars, and over his shoulder was thrown a cloak of ashen gray.

"Would you choose a horse, Sir Siegfried?" asked the stranger.

"Indeed I would," answered he. "But it is hard to make a choice among so many."

"There is one in the meadow," said the man, "far better than all the rest. They say that he came from Odin's pastures on the green hill-slopes of Asgard and that none but the noblest shall ride him."

"Which is he?" asked Siegfried.

"Drive the herd into the river," was the answer, "and then see if you can pick him out."

And Siegfried and the stranger drove the horses down the sloping bank and into the rolling stream; but the flood was too strong for them. Some soon turned back to the shore; while others, struggling madly, were swept away and carried out to the sea. Only one swam safely over. He shook the dripping water from his mane, tossed his head in the air, and then plunged again into the stream. Right bravely he stemmed the torrent the second time. He clambered up the shelving bank and stood by Siegfried's side.

"What need to tell you that this is the horse?" said the stranger. "Take him: he is yours. He is Greyfell, the shining hope that Odin sends to his chosen heroes."

And then Siegfried noticed that the horse's mane glimmered and flashed like a thousand rays from the sun and that his coat was as white and clear as the fresh-fallen snow on the mountains. He turned to speak to the stranger, but he was nowhere to be seen, and Siegfried bethought him how he had talked with Odin unawares. Then he mounted the noble Greyfell and rode with a light heart across the flowery meadows.

"Whither ridest thou?" cried Gripir the ancient from his doorway among the crags.

"I ride into the wide world," said Siegfried; "but I know not whither. I would right the wrong and help the weak and make myself a name on the earth, as did my kinsmen of yore. Tell me, I pray you, where I shall go; for you are wise, and you know the things which have been, and those which shall befall."

"Ride back to Regin, the master of masters," answered Gripir. "He will tell thee of a wrong to be righted."

And the ancient son of the giants withdrew into his lonely abode; and Siegfried, on the shining Greyfell, rode swiftly away towards the south.

Balmung and Greyfell

Name: _____

I. Vocabulary: Underline the following words in the legend. Define each word and use it in a short sentence below.

○ decked: _____

○ deft: _____

○ temper: _____

○ bespangled: _____

○ Odin: _____

II. Plot: Write a simple sentence or phrase to describe the main actions that take place in each scene.

Wonderful Smith	Balmung is Forged	Greyfell is Chosen
1. _____	1. _____	1. _____
2. _____	2. _____	2. _____
3. _____	3. _____	3. _____

III. Characters: List and briefly describe the main characters in this legend.

_____

_____

_____

IV. Rewrite this legend. Be sure to:

○ Include and underline all of the vocabulary words.

○ Write at least three separate paragraphs.

○ Include the following additional requirements.

○ _____

○ _____

○ _____

The Curse of the Gold

When the earth was still young and men were feeble and few and the Dwarfs were many and strong, the Asa-folk sometimes left their halls in Asgard in order to visit the new-formed mid-world and to see what the short-lived sons of men were doing. Sometimes they came in their own god-like splendor and might; sometimes they came disguised as feeble men folk, with all man's weaknesses and all his passions. And many times did men folk entertain them unawares.

Once on a time Odin came to the mid-world in company with Hoenir and Loki; and the three wandered through many lands, each giving gifts wherever they went. At last they sought the solitude of the forest. Late one afternoon they came to a mountain stream where they saw near the bank an otter lazily making ready to eat a salmon which he had caught. And Loki, ever bent on doing mischief, hurled a stone at the harmless beast and killed him. And he took both the otter and the fish which it had caught and carried them with him as trophies of the day's success.

At nightfall the three huntsmen came to a lone farmhouse and asked for food and shelter during the night.

"Shelter you shall have," said the farmer, whose name was Hreidmar, "But food I have none to give you. Surely huntsmen of skill should not want for food, since the forest teems with game and the streams are full of fish."

Then Loki threw upon the ground the otter and the fish and said, "We have sought in both forest and stream, and we have taken from them both flesh and fish. Give us the shelter you promise, and we will not trouble you for food."

The farmer gazed with horror upon the lifeless body of the otter and cried out, "This creature which you mistook for an otter and which you have robbed and killed is my son Oddar, who for mere pastime had taken the form of the furry beast. You are but thieves and murderers!"

Then he called loudly for help; and his two sons Fafnir and Regin, sturdy and valiant kin of the dwarf-folk, rushed in and seized upon the huntsmen and bound them hand and foot; for the three Asa, having taken upon themselves the forms of men, had no more than human strength and were unable to withstand them.

Then Odin and his fellows bemoaned their ill fate. And Loki said, "Why did we foolishly take upon ourselves the likenesses of men? Had I my own power once more, I would never part with it in exchange for man's weaknesses."

Then they asked Hreidmar, their jailer, what ransom they should pay for their freedom; and he, not knowing who they were, said, "I must first know what ransom you are able to give."

"We will give any thing you may ask," hastily answered Loki.

Hreidmar then called his sons and bade them strip the skin from the otter's body. When this was done, they brought the furry hide and spread it upon the ground; and Hreidmar said, "Bring shining gold and precious stones enough to cover every part of this otter skin. When you have paid so much ransom, you shall have your freedom."

"That we will do," answered Odin, "but one of us must leave to go and fetch it; the other two will stay fast bound until the morning dawns. If, by that time, the gold is not here, you may do with us as you please."

Hreidmar and the two young men agreed to Odin's offer; and, lots being cast, it fell to Loki to go and fetch the treasure. When he had been loosed from the cords which bound him, Loki donned his magic shoes which had carried him over land and sea from the farthest bounds of the mid-world and hastened away upon his errand, until he came to the place where dwelt the swarthy elves and the cunning dwarf Andvari.

Loki came to this place, because he knew that here was the home of the elves who had laid up the greatest hoard of treasures ever known in the mid-world. He scanned with careful eyes the mountain side and the deep, rocky caverns and a dark gorge through which a little river rushed; but in the dim moonlight not a living being could he see, save a lazy salmon swimming in the quieter eddies of the stream. Any one but Loki would have lost all hope of finding treasure there, at least before the dawn of day; but his wits were quick, and his eyes were very sharp.

"One salmon has brought us into this trouble, and another shall help us out of it!" he cried.

Then, swift as thought, he sprang again into the air; and the magic shoes carried him with greater speed than before to Ran the Ocean Queen. From her he borrowed a magic net and turned his face again towards Rhineland; and the magic shoes bore him aloft and carried him in a moment back to the ice mountain and the gorge and the infant river, which he had so lately left. The salmon still rested in his place and had not moved during Loki's short absence.

Loki unfolded the net and cast it into the stream. The cunning fish tried hard to avoid being caught in its meshes; but, dart which way he would, he met the skilfully woven cords, and these drew themselves around him, and held him fast. Then Loki pulled the net up out of the water and grasped the helpless fish in his right hand. But, lo! as he held the struggling creature high in the air, it was no longer a fish but the cunning dwarf Andvari.

"Thou King of the Dwarves," cried Loki, " Tell me, on thy life, where thy hidden treasures lie!"

The wise dwarf knew who it was that thus held him as in a vise; and he answered frankly, for it was his only hope of escape, "Turn over the stone upon which you stand. Beneath it you will find the treasure you seek."

Then Loki put his shoulder to the rock and pushed with all his might. But it seemed as firm as the mountain and would not be moved. So the dwarf put his shoulder to the rock, and it turned over as if by magic, and underneath was disclosed a wondrous chamber whose walls shone brighter than the sun, and on whose floor lay treasures of gold and glittering gem stones such as no man had ever seen. And Loki, in great haste, seized upon the hoard and placed it in the magic net which he had borrowed from the Ocean-queen. Then he came out of the chamber; and Andvari again put his shoulder to the rock which lay at the entrance, and it swung back noiselessly to its place.

"What is that upon thy finger?" suddenly cried Loki. "Wouldst keep back a part of the treasure? Give me the ring thou hast!"

But the dwarf shook his head and made answer, "I have given thee all the riches that the elves of the mountain have gathered since the world began. This ring I cannot give thee, for without its help we shall never be able to gather more treasures together."

And Loki grew angry at these words and tore the ring by force from Andvari's fingers. It was a wondrous little piece, shaped like a serpent, coiled, with its tail in its mouth; and its scaly sides glittered with many a tiny diamond, and its ruby eyes shone with an evil light. When the dwarf knew that Loki really meant to rob him of the ring, he cursed it and all who should ever possess it, saying, "May the ill-gotten treasure that you have seized to-night be your bane, and the bane of all to whom it may come, whether by fair means or by foul! And the ring which you have torn from my hand, may it entail upon the one who wears it sorrow and untold ills, the loss of friends and a violent death thus it must be."

Loki was pleased with these words, for he knew that no curses could ever make his own life more cheerless than it always had been. So he thanked Andvari for his curses and treasures; and, throwing the magic net upon his shoulder, he sprang again into the air and was carried swiftly back to Hunaland; and, just before the dawn appeared, he alighted at the door of the farmhouse where Odin and Hoenir still lay bound and guarded by Fafnir and Regin.

Then the farmer, Hreidmar, brought the otter's skin and spread it upon the ground; and, lo! it grew and spread out on all sides, until it covered an acre of ground. And he cried out, "Fulfill now your promise! Cover every hair of this hide with gold or with precious stones. If you fail to do this, then your lives, by your own agreement, are forfeited.

Odin took the magic net from Loki's shoulder; and, opening it, he poured the treasures of the mountain-dwarfs upon the otter skin. And Loki and Hoenir spread the yellow pieces carefully and evenly over every part of the furry hide. But, after every piece had been laid in its place, Hreidmar saw near the otter's mouth a single hair uncovered; and he declared, that unless this hair, too, were covered, the bargain would be unfulfilled, and the treasures and lives of his prisoners would be forfeited. And the Asar looked at each other in dismay; for not another piece of gold and not another precious stone could they find in the net, although they searched with greatest care. At last Odin took from his bosom the ring which Loki had stolen from the dwarf; for he had been so highly pleased with its form and workmanship that he had hidden it, hoping that it would not be needed to complete the payment of the ransom. And they laid the ring upon the uncovered hair. And now no portion of the otter's skin could be seen. And Fafnir and Regin, the ransom being paid, loosed the shackles of Odin and Hoenir and bade the three huntsmen go their way.

Odin and Hoenir at once shook off their human disguises and, taking their own forms again, hastened with all speed back to Asgard. But Loki tarried a little while and said to Hreidmar and his sons, "By your greediness and falsehood you have won for yourselves the Curse of the Earth, which lies before you. It shall be the bane of every one who holds it. It shall make you mean, selfish, beastly. It shall transform you into monsters. Such is gold, and such it shall ever be to its worshipers. And the ring which you have gotten shall impart to its possessor its own nature. Grasping, snaky, cold, unfeeling, shall he live; and death through treachery shall be his doom."

Then he turned away, delighted that he had thus left the curse of Andvari with Hreidmar and his sons and hastened northward toward the sea; for he wished to return to the Ocean queen her magic net.

No sooner were the strange huntsmen well out of sight than Fafnir and Regin began to ask their father to divide the glittering hoard with them. "By our strength and through our advice," said they, "this great store has come into your hands. Let us place it in three equal heaps, and then let each take his share and go his way."

At this the farmer waxed very angry; and he loudly declared that he would keep all the treasure for himself and that his sons should not have any portion of it whatever. So Fafnir and Regin, nursing their disappointment, went to the fields to watch their sheep; but their father sat down to guard his new-gotten treasure. And he took in his hand the glittering serpent ring and gazed into its cold ruby eyes; and, as he gazed, all his thoughts were fixed upon his gold. And behold, as he continued to look at the snaky ring, a dreadful change came over him. His warm red blood became purple and cold and sluggish; and selfishness, like serpent's poison, took hold of his heart. Then, as he kept on gazing at the hoard which lay before him, he began to lose his human shape: his body lengthened into many scaly folds, and he coiled himself around his loved treasures - the very likeness of the ring upon which he had looked so long.

When the day drew near its close, Fafnir came back from the fields with his herd of sheep and thought to find his father guarding the treasure, but instead he saw a glittering snake, fast asleep, encircling the hoard like a huge scaly ring of gold. His first thought was that the monster had devoured his father; and, hastily drawing his sword, with one blow severed the serpent's head from its body. And, while the creature writhed in the death-agony, he gathered up the hoard and fled with it until he came to a barren heath far from the homes of men. There he placed the treasures in one glittering heap and then he gazed with greedy eyes upon the fateful ring, until he, too, was changed into a cold and slimy reptile. And he coiled himself about the hoard; and, with his restless eyes forever open, he gloated day after day upon his gold and watched with ceaseless care that no one should come near to despoil him of it. This was ages and ages ago; and still Fafnir the dragon wallows among his treasures on the Glittering Heath until a hero shall come to slay him.

The Curse of the Gold

Name: _____

I. Vocabulary: Underline the following words in the legend. Define each word and use it in a short sentence below.

○ donned: _____

○ eddies: _____

○ bane: _____

○ forfeited: _____

○ ransom: _____

II. Plot: Write a simple sentence or phrase to describe the main actions that take place in each scene.

Oddar the Otter

1. _____

2. _____

3. _____

Lo, it Grew!

1. _____

2. _____

3. _____

Fateful Ring

1. _____

2. _____

3. _____

III. Characters: List and briefly describe the main characters in this legend.

_____

_____

_____

IV. Rewrite this legend. Be sure to:

○ Include and underline all of the vocabulary words.

○ Write at least three separate paragraphs.

○ Include the following additional requirements.

38

Fafnir, the Dragon

I

Early one morning, Siegfried mounted his horse Greyfell and rode out with Regin, the master smith. They went to slay the dragon Fafnir and gain for Regin the hoard which Fafnir guarded. For seven days they wended their way through the thick greenwood. On the eighth day they came to the open country and to the hills where the land was covered with black boulders and broken by yawning chasms. And no living thing was seen there, not even an insect nor a blade of grass; and the silence of the grave was over all. But Siegfried rode onwards in the way which Regin pointed out and faltered not, although he grew faint with thirst and with the overpowering heat. Towards the evening of the next day they came to a dark mountain wall which stretched far out on either hand and rose high above them, so steep that it seemed to close up the way and to forbid them going farther.

"This is the wall!" cried Regin. "Beyond this mountain is the Glittering Heath and the goal of all my hopes."

And the little old man ran forward and scaled the rough side of the mountain and reached its summit, while Siegfried and Greyfell were yet toiling among the rocks at its foot. Slowly and painfully they climbed the steep ascent. The sun at last went down, and one by one the stars came out; and the moon was rising when Siegfried stood by Regin's side and gazed from the mountain-top down upon the Glittering Heath which lay beyond. And a strange, weird scene it was that met his sight. At the foot of the mountain was a river, white and cold and still; and beyond it was a smooth and barren plain, lying silent in the pale moonlight. But in the distance was seen a circle of flickering flames, ever changing, now growing brighter, now fading away, and now shining with a dull, cold light. As Siegfried gazed upon the scene, he saw the dim outline of some hideous monster moving hither and thither and seeming all the more terrible in the uncertain light.

"It is he!" whispered Regin, and his lips were ashy pale and his knees trembled beneath him. "It is Fafnir! Shall we not go back to the smithy and to the life of ease and safety that may be ours there? Or will you rather dare to go forward and meet the Terror in its abode?"

"None but cowards give up an undertaking once begun," answered Siegfried. "Go back to Rhineland yourself, if you are afraid; but you must go alone. You have brought me thus far to meet the dragon and to win the hoard of the swarthy elves and to rid the world of a terrible evil. Before the setting of another sun, the deed which you have urged me to do will be done."

II

Then he dashed down the eastern slope of the mountain, leaving Greyfell and the trembling Regin behind him. Soon he stood on the banks of the river, which lay between the mountain and the heath; but the stream was deep and sluggish, and the channel was very wide. He paused a moment, wondering how he should cross; and the air seemed heavy with deadly vapors, and the water was thick and cold. While he thus stood in thought, a boat came silently out of the mists and drew near; and the boatman stood up and called to him and said, "What man are you who dares come into this land of loneliness and fear?"

"I am Siegfried," answered the lad; "and I have come to slay Fafnir, the Terror."

"Sit in my boat," said the boatman, "and I will carry you across the river."

And Siegfried sat by the boatman's side; and without the use of an oar and without a breath of air to drive it forward, the little vessel turned and moved silently towards the farther shore.

"In what way will you fight the dragon?" asked the boatman.

"With my trusty sword Balmung I shall slay him," answered Siegfried.

"But he breathes deathly poisons and no man can withstand his strength," said the boatman.

"I will find some way by which to overcome him."

"Then be wise and listen to me," said the boatman. "As you go up from the river you will find a road, worn deep and smooth, starting from the water's edge and winding over the moor. It is the trail of Fafnir, down which he comes at dawn of every day to slake his thirst at the river. Dig a pit in this roadway, a pit narrow and deep, and hide yourself within it. In the morning, when Fafnir passes over it, let him feel the edge of Balmung."

As the man ceased speaking, the boat touched the shore, and Siegfried leaped out. He looked back to thank his unknown friend, but neither boat nor boatman was to be seen. Only a thin white mist rose slowly from the cold surface of the stream. Then, with a braver heart than before, he went forward, along the river bank, until he came to Fafnir's trail, a deep, wide furrow in the earth, beginning at the river's bank and winding far away over the heath, until it was lost to sight in the darkness. The bottom of the trail was soft and slimy, and its sides had been worn smooth by Fafnir's frequent travel through it.

In this road, at a point not far from the river, Siegfried, with his trusty sword Balmung, scooped out a deep and narrow pit, as he had been directed. And when the gray dawn began to appear in the east he hid himself within this trench and waited for the coming of the monster. He had not long to wait; for no sooner had the sky begun to redden in the light of the coming sun than the dragon was heard bestirring himself. Siegfried peeped warily from his hiding place and saw him coming far down the road, hurrying with all speed, that he might quench his thirst at the sluggish river and hasten back to his gold; and the sound which he made was like the trampling of many feet and the jingling of many chains. With bloodshot eyes and gaping mouth and flaming nostrils, the hideous creature came rushing onwards.

His sharp, curved claws dug deep into the soft earth; and his bat-like wings, half trailing on the ground, half flapping in the air, made a sound like that which is heard when Thor rides in his goat-drawn chariot over the dark thunder clouds. It was a terrible moment for Siegfried, but still he was not afraid. He crouched low down in his hiding place, and the bare blade of the trusty Balmung glittered in the morning light. On came the hastening feet and the flapping wings: the red gleam from the monster's flaming nostrils lighted up the trench where Siegfried lay. He heard a roaring and a rushing like the sound of a whirlwind in the forest; then a black, inky mass rolled above him, and all was dark. Now was Siegfried's opportunity. The bright edge of Balmung gleamed in the darkness one moment, and then it smote the heart of Fafnir as he passed. Some men say that Odin sat in the pit with Siegfried and strengthened his arm and directed his sword or else he could not thus have slain the Terror. But, be this as it may, the victory was soon won. The monster stopped short, while but half of his long body had glided over the pit; for sudden death had overtaken him. His horrid head fell lifeless upon the ground; his cold wings flapped once and then lay, quivering and helpless, spread out on either side; and streams of thick black blood flowed from his heart, through the wound beneath, and filled the trench in which Siegfried was hidden and ran like a mountain torrent down the road towards the river. Siegfried was covered from head to foot with the slimy liquid, and, had he not quickly leaped from his hiding place, he would have been drowned in the swift-rushing stream.

III

The bright sun rose in the east and gilded the mountain tops and fell upon the still waters of the river and lighted up the treeless plains around. The south wind played gently against Siegfried's cheeks and in his long hair, as he stood gazing on his fallen foe. And the sound of singing birds and rippling waters and gay insects, such as had not broken the silence of the Glittering Heath for ages, came to his ears. The Terror was dead, and Nature had awakened from her sleep of dread. And as the lad leaned upon his sword and thought of the deed he had done, behold! the shining Greyfell, with the beaming, hopeful mane, having crossed the now bright river, stood by his side. And Regin, his face grown wondrous cold, came trudging over the meadows; and his heart was full of guile. Then the mountain vultures came wheeling downward to look upon the dead dragon; and with them were two ravens, black as midnight. And when Siegfried saw these ravens he knew them to be Odin's birds, Hugin, thought, and Munin, memory. And they alighted on the ground near by; and the lad listened to hear what they would say. Then Hugin flapped his wings and said,

"The deed is done. Why tarries the hero?"

And Munin said, "The world is wide. Fame waits for the hero."

Then Hugin flew past his ear and whispered, "Beware of Regin! His heart is poisoned. He will be thy bane."

And the two birds flew away to carry the news to Odin in the happy halls of Gladsheim.

When Regin drew near to look upon the dragon, Siegfried tried to speak to him but he seemed not to hear; and a snaky glitter lurked in his eyes, and his mouth was set and dry, and he seemed as one walking in a dream.

"It is mine now," he murmured: "it is all mine, now, the Hoard of the swarthy elf-folk, the garnered wisdom of ages. The strength of the world is mine. I will keep, I will save, I will heap up; and none shall have part or parcel of the treasure which is mine alone."

Then his eyes fell upon Siegfried; and his cheeks grew dark with wrath and he cried out, "Why are you here in my way? I am the lord of the Glittering Heath; I am the master of the Hoard and you are my thrall."

Siegfried wondered at the change which had taken place in his old master; but he only smiled at his strange words and made no answer.

"You have slain my brother!" Regin cried; and his face grew fearfully black, and his mouth foamed with rage.

"I have rid the world of a Terror; I have righted a grievous wrong," calmly answered Siegfried.

"You have slain my brother," said Regin; "and a murderer's ransom you shall pay!"

"Take the Hoard for your ransom, and let us each wend his way," said the lad.

"The Hoard is mine by rights," answered Regin still more wrathfully.

Then, blinded with madness, he rushed at Siegfried as if to strike him down; but his foot slipped in a puddle of gore, and he pitched headlong against the sharp edge of Balmung. So sudden was this movement that the sword was twitched out of Siegfried's hand and fell with a dull splash into the blood filled pit before him; while Regin, slain by his own rashness, sank dead upon the ground. Full of horror, Siegfried turned away and mounted Greyfell.

"This is a place of blood," said he, "and the way to glory leads not through it. Let the Hoard still lie on the Glittering Heath; I will go my way hence; and the world shall know me for better deeds than this."

And he turned his back on the fearful scene, and rode away swiftly.

40

Fafnir, the Dragon

Name: _____

I. Vocabulary: Underline the following words in the legend. Define each word and use it in a short sentence below.

○ wended: _____

○ hideous: _____

○ abode _____

○ warily: _____

○ guile: _____

II. Plot: Write a simple sentence or phrase to describe the main actions that take place in each scene.

Glittering Heath	The Terror	Place of Blood
1. _____	1. _____	1. _____
2. _____	2. _____	2. _____
3. _____	3. _____	3. _____

III. Characters: List and briefly describe the main characters in this legend.

_____

_____

_____

IV. Rewrite this legend. Be sure to:

○ Include and underline all of the vocabulary words.

○ Write at least three separate paragraphs.

○ Include the following additional requirements.

41

In Nibelungen Land

I

Once in his adventures Siegfried came to Nibelungen Land where the light of the sun was not strong enough to scatter the fogs and thick vapors that rested upon the land. Siegfried rode on until he came to the steep side of a shadowy mountain. There, at the mouth of a cavern, a strange sight met his eyes. Two young men, dressed in princes' clothing, sat upon the ground; their features were all haggard and gaunt and pinched with hunger, and their eyes wild with wakefulness and fear; and all around them were heaps of gold and precious stones - more than a hundred wagons could carry. And neither of the two princes would leave the shining hoard for food or close his eyes in sleep lest the other might seize and hide some part of the treasure. And thus they had watched and hungered through many long days and sleepless nights, each hoping that the other would die and that the whole inheritance might be his own.

When they saw Siegfried riding near, they called out to him and said, "Noble stranger, stop a moment! Come and help us divide this treasure."

"Who are you?" asked Siegfried, "and what treasure is it lies there?"

"We are the sons of Niblung, who until lately was king of this Mist Land. Our names are Schilbung and the young Niblung," faintly answered the princes.

"And what are you doing here with this gold and these glittering stones?"

"This is the great Nibelungen Hoard, which our father not long ago brought from the Southland. Our father is now dead, and we have brought the hoard out of the cavern where he had hidden it in order that we may share it between us equally. But we cannot agree, and we pray you to help us divide it."

Then Siegfried dismounted from the horse Greyfell and came near the two princes.

"I will gladly do as you ask," said he, "but first I must know more about your father - who he was and whether this is really the Hoard of the Glittering Heath."

Then Niblung answered, as well as his feeble voice would allow, "Our father was, from the earliest times, the ruler of this land and the lord of the fog and the mist. But he did more than rule over the Nibelungen Land. Twice every year he crossed the sea and rambled through the Rhine valleys or loitered in the moist Lowlands, and now and then he brought rich trophies back to his island home. The last time, he brought this treasure with him, but, as we have said, it is not clear how he obtained it. We have heard men say that it was the Hoard of Andvari and that when Fafnir, the dragon who watched it, was slain, the hero who slew him left it to be taken again by the swarthy elves who had gathered it; but because of a curse which Andvari had placed upon it, no one would touch it, until some man would assume its ownership and take upon himself the risk of incurring the curse. This thing, it is said, our father did. And the dwarf Alberich undertook to keep it for him; and he, with the help of the ten thousand elves who live in these caverns and the twelve giants whom you see standing on the mountain peaks around, guarded it faithfully so long as our father lived. But, when he died, we and our thralls fetched it forth from the cavern and spread it here on the ground. And, lo! for many days we have watched and tried to divide it equally. But we cannot agree."

"What hire will you give me if I divide it for you?" asked Siegfried.

"Name what you will have," answered the princes.

"Give me the sword which lies before you on the glittering heap."

Then Niblung handed him the sword and said, "Right gladly will we give it. It is a worthless blade that our father brought from the Southland. They say that he found it also on the Glittering Heath, in the trench where Fafnir was slain. But it is of no use to us, for it turns against us whenever we try to use it."

Siegfried took the sword. It was his own Balmung that had been lost so long.

II

Forthwith he began the task of dividing the treasure; and the two brothers, so faint from hunger and want of sleep that they could scarcely lift their heads, watched him with anxious, greedy eyes. First he placed a piece of gold by Niblung's side, and then a piece of like value he gave to Schilbung. And this he did again and again until no more gold was left. Then, in the same manner, he divided the precious gem stones until none remained. And the brothers were much pleased; and they hugged their glittering treasures and thanked Siegfried for his kindness and for the fairness with which he had given to each his own. But one thing was left which had not fallen to the lot of either brother. It was a ring of curious workmanship - a serpent coiled with its tail in its mouth and with ruby eyes glistening and cold.

"What shall I do with this ring?" asked Siegfried.

"Give it to me!"" cried Niblung.

"Give it to me!"" cried Schilbung.

And both tried to snatch it from Siegfried's hand.

But the effort was too great for the starved, sleepless brothers. Their arms fell helpless at their sides, their feet slipped beneath them, and their limbs failed: they sank fainting, each upon his pile of treasures.

"O my dear, dear gold!" murmured Niblung, trying to clasp it all in his arms, "my dear, dear gold! Thou art mine, mine only. No one shall take thee from me. O my dear, dear gold!" And then, calling up the last spark of life left in his famished body, he cried out to Siegfried, "Give me the ring! The ring I say!"

He hugged his cherished gold nearer to his bosom and pressed his pale lips to the cold and senseless metal as he whispered faintly, "My dear, dear gold!" Then he died.

"O precious, precious gem stones," faltered Schilbung, "how beautiful you are! And you are mine, all mine. Come, come, my bright-eyed beauties! No one but me shall touch you. You are mine, mine, mine!" and he chattered and laughed as only madmen laugh. And he kissed the hard stones and sought to hide them in his bosom. But his hands trembled and failed, dark mists swam before his eyes; and he fancied that he heard the black dwarfs clamoring for his treasure; he sprang up quickly, he shrieked - and then fell lifeless upon his hoard of sparkling gems.

A strange, sad sight it was, boundless wealth and miserable death; two piles of yellow gold and sunbright diamonds and two thin, starved corpses stretched upon them. Some stories relate that the brothers were slain by Siegfried because their foolish strife and greediness had angered him. But I like not to think so. It was the gold, and not Siegfried, that slew them.

"O gold, gold!" cried the hero sorrowfully, "truly thou art the mid-world's curse; thou art man's bane."

III

But Siegfried had little time for thought and speech. Alberich the dwarf, the master of the swarthy elves who guarded the Nibelungen Hoard, had come out from his cavern and seen the two princes lying dead beside their treasures, and he thought that they had been murdered by Siegfried. Thus he lifted a little silver horn to his lips and blew a shrill bugle call. At this, little brown elves came trooping forth by thousands: from under every rock, from the nooks and crannies and crevices in the mountain side, from the deep cavern and the narrow gorge, they came at the call of their chief. Then, at Alberich's word, they formed in line of battle and stood in order around the hoard and the bodies of their late masters. Their little golden shields and their sharp-pointed spears were thick as the blades of grass in a Rhine meadow. And Siegfried, when he saw them, was pleased and surprised; for never before had such a host of pygmy warriors stood before him.

While he paused and looked, the elves became suddenly silent, and Siegfried noticed that Alberich stood no longer at their head but had strangely vanished from sight.

"Ah, Alberich!" cried the hero. "Thou art indeed cunning. I have heard of thy tricks. Thou hast donned the Tarnkappe, the cloak of darkness, which hides thee from sight and makes thee as strong as twelve common men. But come on, thou brave dwarf!"

Scarcely had he spoken, when he felt a shock which almost sent him reeling from his saddle and made Greyfell plunge about with fright. Quickly, then, did Siegfried dismount, and, with every sense alert, he waited for the second onset of the unseen dwarf. It was plain that Alberich wished to strike him unawares, for many minutes passed in utter silence. Then a brisk breath of wind passed by Siegfried's face, and he felt another blow; but, by a quick downward movement of his hand, he caught the plucky elf-king and tore off the magic Tarnkappe, and then, with firm grasp, he held him, struggling in vain to get free.

"Ah, Alberich!" he cried, "now I know thou art cunning. But the Tarnkappe I must have for my own. What wilt thou give for thy freedom?"

"Worthy prince," answered Alberich humbly, "you have fairly overcome me in fight and made me your prisoner. I and all mine, as well as this treasure, rightfully belong to you. We are yours, and you we shall obey."

"Swear it!" said Siegfried. "Swear it, and thou shalt live and be the keeper of my treasures."

And Alberich made a sign to his elfin host, and every spear was turned point downwards and every tiny shield was thrown to the ground, and the ten thousand little warriors kneeled, as did also their chief, and acknowledged Siegfried to be their rightful master and the lord of the Nibelungen Land and the owner of the Hoard of Andvari.

Then, by Alberich's orders, the elves carried the Hoard back into the cavern, and there kept faithful watch and ward over it. And they buried the starved bodies of the two princes on the top of the mist-veiled mountain; and heralds were sent to all the strongholds in Nibelungen Land, proclaiming that Siegfried, through his wisdom and might, had become the true lord and king of the land. Afterwards the prince, riding on the beaming Greyfell, went from place to place, scattering sunshine and smiles where shadows and frowns had been before. And the Nibelungen folk welcomed him everywhere. And the pure brightness of his hero-soul and the gleaming sunbeams from Greyfell's mane lifted the curtain of mists and fogs that had so long darkened the land and let in the glorious glad light of day and the genial warmth of summer.

In Nibelungen Land

Name: _____

I. Vocabulary: Underline the following words in the legend. Define each word and use it in a short sentence below.

○ haggard: _____

○ gaunt: _____

○ thralls: _____

○ bane: _____

○ pygmy: _____

II. Plot: Write a simple sentence or phrase to describe the main actions that take place in each scene.

Hoard Discovered	Curious Workmanship	TarnKappe
1. _____	1. _____	1. _____
2. _____	2. _____	2. _____
3. _____	3. _____	3. _____

III. Characters: List and briefly describe the main characters in this legend.

_____

_____

_____

IV. Rewrite this legend. Be sure to:

○ Include and underline all of the vocabulary words.

○ Write at least three separate paragraphs.

○ Include the following additional requirements.

○ _____

○ _____

○ _____

44

Siegfried's Arrival in Burgundy

I

Dankrat and Ute, King and Queen of Burgundy, were the fortunate parents of four children: three sons, Gunther, Gernot, and Giselher; and one beautiful daughter, Kriemhild. When king Dankrat died, his eldest son, Gunther, succeeded him and reigned wisely and well, residing at Worms on the Rhine, his capital and favorite city.

In those days there flourished farther down the Rhine the kingdom of the Netherlands, governed by Siegmund and Sigelind. Siegmund was a wise ruler and was known for his good deeds. Sigelind was loved by all for her goodness of heart and gentleness. They were very proud of their only son and heir, young Siegfried. Neither king nor queen left anything undone that might contribute to Siegfried's happiness or his skill. He was trained in warlike games and feats of strength. No other youth could run more swiftly or shoot the arrow with surer aim. To celebrate Siegfried's knighthood his parents held a great tournament at Xanten on the Rhine. In jousting and the other games the young prince won all the laurels, although great and tried warriors matched their skill against his in the lists.

The festivities continued for seven whole days and when the guests departed they were all heavily laden with the costly gifts which the king and queen had lavished upon them.

After the departure of all these guests, young Siegfried became restless and sought his parents' presence. Then he told them that he had heard rumors of the beauty and attractions of the princess Kriemhild of Burgundy, and he declared his wish to journey thither to secure her as his wife.

In vain the fond parents tried to prevail upon him to remain quietly at home; at last the young hero insisted so strongly that he finally won their consent to his immediate departure. With eleven companions, all decked out in the richest garments that the queen's chests could furnish, the young prince rode down the Rhine and reached Worms on the seventh day.

As they rode onwards through the meadows and the pleasant farming-lands which lay around the city; and they passed a wonderful garden of roses, said to belong to Kriemhild, the peerless princess of the Rhine country; and at last they halted before the castle gate. So lordly was their bearing, that a company of knights came out to meet them and offered, as the custom was, to take charge of their horses and their shields. But Siegfried asked that they be led at once to King Gunther and his brothers; and, as their stay would not be long, they said they would have no need to part with horses or with shields. Then they followed their guides and rode through the great gateway and into the open court and halted beneath the palace-windows.

And the three brothers - Gunther, Gernot, and Giselher - and their young sister, the matchless Kriemhild, looked down upon them from above and hazarded many guesses as to who the lordly strangers might be. And all the inmates of the castle stood at the doors and windows, or gathered in curious groups in the courtyard, and gazed with open-mouthed wonder upon the rich armor and noble bearing of the heroes. But all eyes were turned most towards Siegfried and the wondrous steed Greyfell. Some of the knights whispered that this was Odin, and some that it was Thor, the thunderer, making a tour through Rhineland.

Only one among all the folk in the castle knew who the hero was who had ridden thus boldly into the heart of Burgundyland. That one was Hagen, the uncle of the three kings and the doughtiest warrior in all Rhineland. With a dark drown and a sullen scowl he looked out upon the little party and already plotted in his mind how he might outwit and bring to grief the youth whose name and fame were known the whole world over. For his evil mind loved deeds of darkness and hated the pure and good. By his side, at an upper window, stood Kriemhild, the peerless maiden of the Rhine and others, but none but Hagen knew who the stranger was. At last as the others speculated among themselves Hagen spoke up. "I think I know who this stranger is. He is the knight Siegfried of Burgundy."

The others looked at each other in wonder and asked, "And who is this Siegfried?"

II

"Siegfried," answered Sir Hagen, "is a truly wonderful knight. Once when riding all alone, he came to a mountain where lay the treasure of the king of the Nibelungs. The king's two sons had brought it out from the cave in which it had been hidden, to divide it between them. But they did not agree about the division. So when Siegfried drew near both princes said, 'Divide for us, Sir Siegfried, our father's hoard.' There were so many jewels that one hundred wagons could not carry them, and of ruddy gold there was even more. Seigfied made the fairest division he could, and as a reward the princes gave him their father's sword called Balmung. But although Siegfried had done his best to satisfy them with his division, they soon fell to quarreling and fighting, and when he tried to separate them they made an attack on him. To save his own life he slew them both. Alberich, a mountain dwarf, who had long been guardian of the Nibelung hoard, rushed to avenge his masters; but Siegfried vanquished him and took from him his cap of darkness, or Tarnkappe, which made its wearer invisible and gave him the strength of twelve men. The hero then ordered Alberich to place the treasure again in the mountain cave and guard it for him."

Hagen then told another story of Siegfried.

"Once he slew a fierce dragon and bathed himself in its blood, and this turned the hero's skin to horn, so that no sword or spear can wound him."

Meanwhile the three kings and their chiefs had gone into the courtyard to greet their unknown guests. Very kindly did Gunther welcome the strangers to his home; and then he courteously asked them whence they came and what were the favors they wished.

"I have heard," answered Siegfried, "that many knights and heroes live in this land and that they are the bravest and the proudest in the world. I, too, am a knight; and some time, if I am worthy, I shall be a king. But first I would make good my right to rule over land and folk; and for this reason I have come hither. If, indeed, you are as brave as all the world says you are, ride now to the meadows with us, and let us fight man to man; and he who wins shall rule over the lands of both. We will wager our kingdom and our heads against yours."

King Gunther and his brothers were amazed at this unlooked-for speech.

"Such is not the way to try where true worth lies!" they cried. "We have no cause of quarrel with you, neither have you any cause of quarrel with us. Why then should we spill each other's blood?"

Again Siegfried urged them to fight with him; but they flatly refused. And Gernot said, "The Burgundian kings have never wished to rule over folk that are not their own. Much less would they gain new lands at the cost of their best heroes' blood. And they have never taken part in needless quarrels. Good men in Burgundy are worth more than the broadest lands, and we will not hazard the one for the sake of gaining the other. No, we will not fight. But we greet you most heartily as our friends and guests."

All the others joined in urging Siegfried and his comrades to dismount from their steeds and partake of the cheer with which it was their use to entertain strangers. And at last he yielded to their kind wishes and alighted from Greyfell, and, grasping King Gunther's hand, he made himself known. And there was great rejoicing in the castle and throughout all the land; and the most sumptuous rooms were set apart for the use of Siegfried and his knights; and a banquet was at once made ready; and no pains were spared in giving the strangers a right hearty welcome to the kingly halls of Burgundy.

Siegfried sojourned for nearly a year at Gunther's court, displaying his skill in all martial exercises; and although he never caught a glimpse of the fair maiden Kriemhild, she often admired his strength and manly beauty from behind the palace lattice.

III

One day the games were interrupted by the arrival of a herald announcing that the King of the Saxons and the King of Denmark were about to invade Burgundy. These tidings filled Gunther's heart with terror, for the enemy were very numerous and their valor was beyond all question. But when Hagen hinted that perhaps Siegfried would lend them a helping hand, the King of Burgundy seized the suggestion with joy.

As soon as Siegfried was made aware of the threatened invasion, he declared that if Gunther would only give him one thousand brave men he would repel the foe. This offer was too good to refuse so Gunther hastily assembled a chosen corps.

This little force, only one thousand strong, then marched bravely out of Worms, passed through Hesse, and entered Saxony, where it encountered the enemy numbering no less than twenty thousand valiant fighting men. The battle was immediately begun; and while all fought bravely, none did such wonders as Siegfried, who made both kings prisoners, routed their host, and returned triumphant to Worms, with much spoil and many captives.

A messenger had preceded him thither to announce the success of the expedition, and he was secretly summoned and questioned by Kriemhild, who, in joy at hearing that Siegfried was unharmed and victorious, gave the messenger a large reward.

Kriemhild then hastened to her window, from whence she witnessed her hero's triumphant entrance, and heard the people's acclamations of joy. The wounded were cared for, the captive king's hospitably entertained and duly released, and great festivities were held to celebrate the glorious victory. Among other entertainments the knights tilted in the tournaments, and all the court ladies were invited to view the prowess of the men at arms. It was thus that Siegfried first beheld Kriemhild, and as soon as he saw her he gladly acknowledged that she was fairer than he could ever have supposed.

Siegfried's happiness was complete, however, when he was appointed the escort of this peerless maiden; and on the way to and from the tournament and mass he made good use of his opportunity to whisper pretty speeches to Kriemhild, who timidly expressed her gratitude for the service he had rendered her brother and begged that he would continue to befriend him.

The festivities being ended, Gunther bestowed many gifts on the departing guests; but when Siegfried would also have departed he entreated him to remain at Worms. This the young hero was not at all loath to do, as he had fallen deeply in love with the fair Kriemhild, whom he was now privileged to see every day.

Siegfried's Arrival in Burgundy

I. Vocabulary: Underline the following words in the legend. Define each word and use it in a short sentence below.

○ laurels: _____

○ vanquished: _____

○ martial: _____

○ corps: _____

○ peerless: _____

II. Plot: Write a simple sentence or phrase to describe the main actions that take place in each scene.

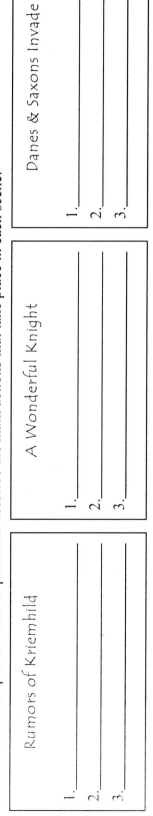

Rumors of Kriemhild

1. _____
2. _____
3. _____

A Wonderful Knight

1. _____
2. _____
3. _____

Danes & Saxons Invade

1. _____
2. _____
3. _____

III. Characters: List and briefly describe the main characters in this legend.

_____

_____

_____

IV. Rewrite this legend. Be sure to:

○ Include and underline all of the vocabulary words.

○ Write at least three separate paragraphs.

○ Include the following additional requirements.

○ _____

○ _____

○ _____

Gunther and Brunhild

I

Far over the sea from sunny Burgundy lived Brunhild, Queen of Iceland. Fair was she of face and strong beyond compare. If a knight would woo and win her he must surpass her in three contests: leaping, hurling the spear, and pitching the stone. If he failed in even one, he must forfeit his life.

King Gunther resolved to wed this strange princess and declared his desire to win her to Siegfried. In vain Siegfried, who knew all about Brunhild, tried to dissuade him; Gunther insisted upon departing but proposed to Siegfried to accompany him, promising him as a reward for his assistance Kriemhild's hand as soon as the princess of Iceland was won. Such an offer was not to be refused, and Siegfried immediately accepted it, advising Gunther to take only Hagen and Dankwart as his attendants.

After seeking the aid of Kriemhild for a supply of rich clothing suitable for a prince going a-wooing, Gunther and the three knights embarked on a small vessel, whose sails soon filled and which rapidly bore them down the Rhine and over the sea to Iceland. When within sight of its shores, Siegfried bade his companions all carefully agree in representing him to the strangers as Gunther's vassal only. Their arrival was seen by some inquisitive damsels peering out of the windows of the castle and reported to Brunhild, who immediately and joyfully concluded that Siegfried had come to seek her hand in marriage. But when she heard that he held another man's stirrup to enable him to mount, she angrily frowned, wondering why he came as a menial instead of as a king. When the strangers entered her hall she would have greeted Siegfried first had he not modestly drawn aside, declaring that the honor was due to his master, Gunther, King of Burgundy, who had come to Iceland to woo her.

Brunhild then haughtily bade her warriors make all the necessary preparations for the coming contest; and Gunther, Hagen, and Dankwart apprehensively watched the movements of four warriors staggering beneath the weight of Brunhild's ponderous shield. Then they saw three others equally overpowered by her spear; and twelve sturdy servants could scarcely roll the stone she was wont to cast.

Hagen and Dankwart, fearing for their master, who was doomed to die in case of failure, began to mutter that some treachery was afoot, and openly regretted that they had consented to lay aside their weapons upon entering the castle. These remarks, overheard by Brunhild, called forth her scorn, and she contemptuously bade her servants bring the strangers' arms, since they were afraid.

While these preliminaries were being settled, Siegfried had gone down to the ship riding at anchor, and all unseen had donned his magic cap, Tarnkappe, and returned to the scene of the coming contest, where he now bade Gunther rely upon his aid and make the gestures as he did the work.

In obedience to these directions, Gunther merely made the motions, depending upon the invisible Siegfried to parry and make all the attacks. Brunhild first poised and flung her spear with such force that both heroes staggered and almost fell; but before she could cry out victory, Siegfried had caught the spear, turned it butt end foremost, and flung it back with such violence that the princess fell and was obliged to acknowledge herself outdone.

Nothing daunted, however, by this first defeat, she caught up the massive stone, flung it far from her, and leaping after it, alighted beside it. But even while she was inwardly congratulating herself and confidently cherishing the belief that the stranger could not surpass her, Siegfried caught up the stone, flung it farther still, and grasping Gunther by his broad girdle, bounded through the air with him and landed far beyond it. Brunhild was outdone in all three feats, and, according to her own promise, belonged to the victor, Gunther, to whom she now bade her people show all due respect and homage.

II

The warriors all hastened to do her bidding and escorted their new lord to the castle, wither, under pretext of fitly celebrating her marriage, Brunhild summoned all her retainers from far and near. This rally roused the secret terror of Gunther, Hagen, and Dankwart, for they suspected some act of treachery on the part of the dark-browed queen. These fears were also, in a measure, shared by Siegfried; so he stole away, promising to return before long with a force sufficient to overawe Brunhild and quell all attempt at foul play.

Siegfried, having hastily embarked upon the little vessel, swiftly sailed away to the Nibelungen land, where he arrived in an incredibly short space of time, and presented himself at the gates of his castle. Then, making himself known to his followers, the Nibelungs, he chose one thousand of them to accompany him back to Iceland to support the Burgundian king.

The arrival of this unexpected force greatly surprised Brunhild. She questioned Gunther, and upon receiving the careless reply that they were only a few of his followers who had come to make merry at his wedding, she gave up all hope of resistance. When the usual festivities had taken place, Gunther bade his bride prepare to follow him back to the Rhine with her personal female attendants who numbered no less than one hundred and sixty-eight.

Brunhild regretfully left her own country, escorted by the thousand Nibelung warriors; and when they had journeyed nine days, Gunther bade Siegfried spur ahead and announce his safe return to his family and subjects.

Kriemhild received this messenger most graciously and gave immediate orders for a magnificent reception of the new queen, going down to the river to meet and greet her in the most cordial and affectionate manner.

A tournament and banquet ensued; but as they were about to sit down to the latter, the impatient Siegfried ventured to remind Gunther of his promise and claim the hand of Kriemhild. In spite of a low-spoken remonstrance on Brunhild's part, who said that he would surely never consent to give his only sister in marriage to a menial, Gunther sent for Kriemhild, who blushingly expressed her readiness to marry Siegfried. The marriage was immediately celebrated, and the two bridal couples sat side by side. But while Kriemhild's fair face was radiant with joy, Brunhild's dark brows were drawn close together in an unmistakable and ominous frown.

III

The banquet over, the newly married couples retired; but when Gunther, for the first time alone with his wife, would fain have embraced her, she seized him and, in spite of his vigorous resistance, bound him fast with her long girdle, suspended him from a nail in the corner of her apartment, and, notwithstanding his piteous entreaties, let him remain there all night long, releasing him only a few moments before the attendants entered the nuptial chamber in the morning. Of course all seemed greatly surprised to see Gunther's lowering countenance which contrasted oddly with Siegfried's radiant mien; for the latter had won a loving wife and, to show his appreciation of her, had given her as a wedding gift the great Nibelungen hoard.

In the course of the day Gunther managed to draw Siegfried aside and secretly confided to him the shameful treatment he had received at his wife's hands. When Siegfried heard this he offered to don his cap of darkness once more, enter the royal chamber unperceived, and force Brunhild to recognize her husband as her master, and never again make use of her strength against him.

In pursuance of this promise Siegfried suddenly left Kriemhild's side at nightfall, stole unseen into the queen's room, and when she and Gunther had closed the door, he blew out the lights and wrestled with Brunhild until she begged for mercy, promising never to bind him again; for as Siegfried had remained invisible throughout the struggle, she thought it was Gunther who had conquered her.

Still unperceived, Siegfried now took her girdle and ring and stole out of the apartment, leaving Gunther alone with his wife; but, true to her promise, Brunhild ever after treated her husband with due respect, and having once for all been conquered, she entirely lost the fabulous strength which had been her proudest boast and was no more powerful than any other member of her sex.

Gunther & Brunhild

Name: _____

I. Vocabulary: Underline the following words in the legend. Define each word and use it in a short sentence below.

○ forfeit: _____

○ vassal: _____

○ donned: _____

○ ominous: _____

○ mien: _____

II. Plot: Write a simple sentence or phrase to describe the main actions that take place in each scene.

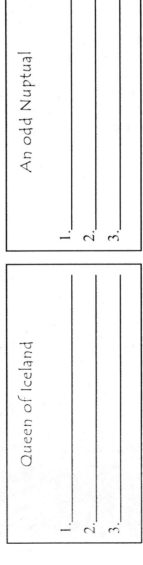

Queen of Iceland
1. _____
2. _____
3. _____

An odd Nuptual
1. _____
2. _____
3. _____

The Taming of Brunhild
1. _____
2. _____
3. _____

III. Characters: List and briefly describe the main characters in this legend.

_____

_____

_____

IV. Rewrite this legend. Be sure to:

○ Include and underline all of the vocabulary words.

○ Write at least three separate paragraphs.

○ Include the following additional requirements.

The Death of Siegfried

I

Ten years had passed since the marriages of Gunther to Brunhild and Siegfried to Kriemhild. During this time Brunhild, still imagining that Siegfried was only her husband's vassal, secretly wondered why he never came to court to do homage for his lands and finally suggested to Gunther that it would be well to invite his sister and her husband to visit them at Worms. Gunther seized this suggestion gladly and immediately sent one of his followers to deliver the invitation which Siegfried accepted for himself and his wife.

On Kriemhild's arrival at Worms, Brunhild greeted her with much pomp and ceremony; but in spite of the amity which seemed to exist between the two queens, Brunhild was secretly angry at what she deemed Kriemhild's unwarrantable arrogance.

One day, when the two queens were sitting together at an upper window, they looked down upon a company of men in the courtyard below. Among them were the noblest earl-folk of Burgundy and Gunther the King and Siegfried. But Siegfried towered above all the rest; and he moved like a god among men.

"See my noble Siegfried!" cried Kriemhild in her pride. "How grandly he stands there! What manly beauty and strength! No one cares to look at other men when he is near."

Brunhild, weary of hearing Kriemhild's constant praise of her husband, cuttingly remarked, "He may be handsome and, for aught I know, he may be noble. But what is all that by the side of kingly power? Were he but the peer of your brother Gunther, then you might well boast."

This remark called forth a retort from Kriemhild, and a dispute was soon raging, in the course of which Kriemhild vowed that she would publicly assert her rank by taking the precedence of Brunhild in entering the church. The queens parted in hot anger, but both immediately proceeded to attire themselves with the utmost magnificence and, escorted by all their maids, met at the church door. Brunhild there bade Kriemhild stand aside and make way for her superior; but this order so angered the Nibelungen queen that the dispute was resumed in public with increased vehemence and bitterness.

In her indignation Kriemhild finally insulted Brunhild grossly by declaring that she was not a faithful wife. In proof of her assertion she produced the ring and girdle which Siegfried had won in his memorable encounter with her and which he had imprudently given to his wife, to whom he had also confided the secret of Brunhild's wooing.

Brunhild indignantly summoned Gunther to defend her, and he, in anger, sent for Siegfried, who publicly swore that his wife had not told the truth and that Gunther's queen had in no way forfeited her good name. Further to propitiate his host, Siegfried declared the quarrel to be disgraceful and promised to teach his wife better manners for the future.

Brunhild, smarting from the public insult, continued to weep aloud and complain, until Hagen, inquiring the cause of her extravagant grief and receiving a highly colored version of the affair, declared that he would see that she was duly avenged.

II

To keep his promise, Hagen tried to stir up the anger of Gunther and his brothers, Gernot and Giselher. Hagen continually reminded Gunther of the insult his wife had received, setting it in the worst possible light, and finally so worked upon the king's feelings that he consented to a treacherous assault.

Under pretext that his former enemy, the King of the Saxons, was about to attack him again, Gunther asked Siegfried's assistance and began to prepare as if for war. When Kriemhild heard that her beloved husband was about to rush into danger she was greatly troubled. Hagen artfully pretended to share her alarm and so won her confidence.

In a moment in weakness Kriemhild confided to Hagen. "I should not fear for him," said she, "if he were not so bold and reckless. When he is in the battle, he never thinks of his own safety. If you knew every thing, as I do, you would fear for him too."

"What is it that gives you cause for fear?" asked Hagen, trying to hide his eagerness. "Tell me all about it, and then I will know the better how to shield him from danger. I will lay down my life for his sake."

Then Kriemhild, trusting in her uncle's word, revealed to him that when Siegfried killed the dragon Fafnir he was covered by the dragon's blood and his skin was made as hard as horn where the blood had covered. Thus Siegfried was invulnerable except in one spot, between his shoulders, where a lime leaf had rested and the dragon's blood had not touched him.

"And now," she added, "since I know that there is one spot which a deadly weapon might reach, I am in constant fear that the spear of an enemy may strike him there. Is there not some way of shielding that spot?"

"There is," answered Hagen. "Make some mark upon his coat that I may know where the spot is. And, when the battle rages, I will ride close behind him and ward off every threatened stroke."

And Kriemhild joyfully promised that she would at once embroider a silken lime leaf on the hero's coat, just over the fatal spot. And Hagen, well pleased, bade her farewell and went away.

When Siegfried joined them on the morrow, wearing the fatal marked doublet, he was surprised to hear that the

51

rebellion had been quelled without a blow; and when invited to join in a hunt, he gladly signified his consent. After bidding farewell to Kriemhild he joined the hunting party. He scoured the forest, slew several boars, a mighty elk, and many deer and stags and savage beasts. He even caught a bear alive.

Soon the call of a bugle was heard, and Gunther and Hagen with their huntsmen and hounds came riding up. "How glad I am," said Siegfried gayly as he spied the others, "that I am not a huntsman by trade, if it is the huntsman's way to go thus dry! Oh for a cup of cold spring water to quench my thirst!"

Then Hagen pointed to a tree not far away, beneath whose spreading branches Siegfried could see the water of a spring sparkling in the sunlight. "Men have told me," said Hagen, "that the Nibelungen king is very fleet of foot and that no one has ever outstripped him in a race. Suppose we try a race to the spring and see who can win?" "Agreed!" cried Siegfried. "We will run; and I will give the odds in your favor. I will carry with me my spear, shield, helmet, and sword while you may doff from your shoulders whatever might hinder your speed."

This challenge was accepted by Hagen and Gunther. Although heavily handicapped, Siegfried reached the spring first. While he bent over to drink Hagen treacherously glided behind him and drove his spear through his body in the exact spot where Kriemhild had embroidered the fatal mark.

Mortally wounded, Siegfried made a desperate effort to avenge himself; but finding nothing but his shield within reach, he flung it with such force at his murderer that it knocked him down. This last effort exhausted the remainder of his strength, and the hero fell back upon the grass, cursing the treachery of those whom he had trusted.

When Siegfried had expired, the hunters silently gathered around his corpse, regretfully contemplating the fallen hero, while they took counsel together how they might keep the secret of Hagen's treachery. They finally agreed to carry the body back to Worms and to say that they had found Siegfried dead in the forest, where he had presumably been slain by highwaymen.

Although his companions were anxious to shield him, Hagen gloried in his dastardly deed and secretly bade the bearers deposit Siegfried's corpse at Kriemhild's door after nightfall, so that she should be the first to see it there when on her way to early Mass. As he fully expected, Kriemhild immediately recognized her husband and fell senseless upon him; but when she had recovered consciousness she declared that Siegfried was the victim of an assassination.

By her orders a messenger was sent to break the mournful tidings to the Nibelungs. They hastily armed and rallied about her and would have fallen upon the Burgundians, had she not restrained them, bidding them wait a suitable occasion.

III

The preparations for a sumptuous funeral were immediately begun, and all lent a willing hand, for Siegfried was greatly beloved at Worms. His body was therefore laid in the cathedral, where all came to view it and condole Kriemhild; but when Gunther drew near to express his sorrow, she refused to listen to him until he promised that all those present at the hunt should touch the body, which at the murderer's contact would bleed afresh. All stood the test and were honorably acquitted save Hagen, at whose touch Siegfried's blood began to flow.

Once more Kriemhild restrained the angry Nibelung warriors and went through the remainder of the funeral ceremonies and saw her hero duly laid at rest.

Kriemhild's mourning had only begun. All her days and nights were now spent in bitter weeping. The Nibelung knights had returned home muttering dark threats and Eckewart the steward alone remained with Kriemhild and prepared a dwelling close by the cathedral for his mistress so that she might daily visit his tomb. Here Kriemhild spent three years in seclusion, refusing to see Gunther or the detested Hagen; but they, remembering that the immense Nibelungen hoard was hers by right, continually wondered how she could be induced to send for it. Owing to Hagen's advice, Gunther, helped by his brothers, finally obtained an interview with, and was reconciled to, his mourning sister. Shortly after he persuaded her to send twelve men to claim from Alberich, the dwarf, the fabulous wealth her husband had bestowed upon her as a wedding gift.

But although this wealth was immense, Kriemhild would have gladly given it all away to once again see her beloved Siegfried. Not knowing what else to do with it, she gave away her gold right and left, bidding all the recipients to pray for Siegfried's soul. Her largesses were so extensive that Hagen sought out Gunther and told him that Kriemhild was secretly winning to her side many adherents, whom she would some day urge to avenge her husband's murder by slaying her kindred.

While Gunther was trying to devise some plan to obtain possession of the hoard, Hagen boldly seized the keys of the tower where it was kept, secretly removed all the gold, and, to prevent its falling into any hands but his own, sank it in the Rhine.

And this was the end of the fated Hoard of Andvari.

The Death of Siegfried

Name: _____

I. Vocabulary: Underline the following words in the legend. Define each word and use it in a short sentence below.

○ homage: _____

○ amity: _____

○ invulnerable: _____

○ condole: _____

○ largesse: _____

II. Plot: Write a simple sentence or phrase to describe the main actions that take place in each scene.

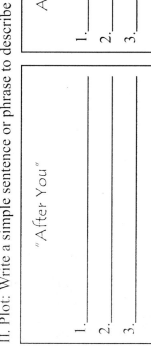

"After You"

1. _____
2. _____
3. _____

Assassination at the Spring

1. _____
2. _____
3. _____

Days of Mourning

1. _____
2. _____
3. _____

III. Characters: List and briefly describe the main characters in this legend.

_____

_____

_____

IV. Rewrite this legend. Be sure to:

○ Include and underline all of the vocabulary words.

○ Write at least three separate paragraphs.

○ Include the following additional requirements.

_____

_____

_____

St. George and the Dragon

I

The King of Selene, a city in Libya, had one daughter, named Cleodolinda.

Cleodolinda was a sweet maid. Her form was fair, her eyes were clear and lustrous, and her heart was pure. She was as sweet as a summer morning and as brave as a winter sun.

The King loved this Princess with a great love. She was dearer to him than aught else in the world. And when Cleodolinda was fourteen years of age, the King thought he had never seen anything more beautiful than she.

One night, as the watchman went round the walls of Selene, he felt upon the air a most poisonous vapor that came from without the walls. And even as he wondered, the fumes of the poison became too much for him and he fell over and in a little time expired.

And in the morning another watchman, making his round, found this fellow dead beside the city. And upon the air was a faint odor that was unpleasant to the nostrils. Then the watchman scaled the wall, and, having glanced over, he perceived a huge beast which crawled away from the city and toward the marshes. As it crawled it flapped two great black wings, and from its nostrils belched out a black flame which contained those poisonous fumes of which the watchman felt the trace. Its body was covered with scales so strong and smooth that they were like a knight's armor; and in shape it was half crawling beast half loathsome bird. As the watchman observed it, the dragon crawled into the farther part of the marshes and lay still.

Then the watchman hurried to those in authority to report this affair; and when the matter came to the King's ears, he gave orders that none should go outside the city walls till the dragon had gone back whence it came. So the long day through no man went outside the city walls, but many adventurous persons, having gained a perch upon the walls, observed the dragon, which had come into the sunlight and could be seen lying there. Then, in the evening, the dragon roused itself and started to crawl toward the city. It crawled on four twisted feet and pushed itself with its wings; and its eyes shone like red flames. As this vile creature approached, the people were afraid and retreated into the city, for they knew not for what purpose the dragon came. When it had reached the gates of the city, it took up a position close to them; and from its nostrils it poured terrible fumes, so that the people were like to die.

Then the King called together his knights, and one who was braver than any other declared that he would discover from the dragon its purpose in so haunting the city. And having entreated the dragon to cease casting out its poison while he spake with it, he approached and asked for what purpose it had come to the gates of Selene.

The dragon replied, by signs and hoarse noises, that it would only depart from the city gates and cease troubling the people of Selene with its poison, if it were granted a meal of two sheep a day. When the King heard of this reply, he ordered that two sheep should be set aside every day for the dragon and put without the city walls. And when the dragon had on that day received two sheep, it devoured them and crawled back to its lair. But it remained in the marshes, and not far from the city, so that none might enter the city or come out of it for fear of the dragon. And every day it roused itself and crawled to the gates to receive its meal of two sheep.

After a time the sheep became few in number, so that there would not long be enough to feed the dragon; and the people were possessed with fear. Then came to the King the bravest knights of Selene, praying him that he would allow them to go out and do battle with the dragon.

II

The King replied to them, "My brave knights, I fear me that ye go to your deaths. Yet can I neither forbid nor dissuade ye, for the fate of my people lies heavy on my heart." Having so spoken he became silent, for the foreboding was upon him that darker trouble was to come upon the people of Selene.

Then went out the knights to do battle with the dragon. And when it perceived them issue from the city gates, it forsook its lair and ran toward them with a most incredible speed. And, having come near, it fell upon them, breathing out its terrible poison and lashing them with its wings. And, since the knights could neither pierce the scales with which its body was covered nor stun the creature with the hardest blow, they were speedily overcome by the fumes that emanated from it. And they perished, one and all.

Then there was weeping in Selene for the fate of the bravest of her knights. And while the people wept, they trembled, for the sheep that remained were few. And the day came when there was no longer one left to offer to the dragon, and it lay again by the city gates and threw its poison into the city.

And the King went to the gates of the city and called upon the dragon to cease its poison for a time since he would talk with it. Then said the King, "Our sheep are all finished, and indeed there is little food of any kind in Selene. Since this be so, wilt not thou leave our gates and return to thine own place?"

But the dragon, lifting its loathly head, made answer, by signs and noises, "I will not return to it. Let me be granted one child a day for my meal, and I will not molest the people of Selene." And it would say no more.

Then the King went back the way he had come, and he walked heavily, for in his breast his heart was turned to stone. And he was filled with one great fear.

Cried the people of Selene, "We care no longer to live, since our children are to be taken from us!"

Nevertheless, because the poison from the dragon was reaching everywhere so that none could escape, they promised, with bitter weeping, to offer up one child a day, hoping that the dragon would return to its home ere all the children were devoured.

And every day lots were cast. And upon whom fell the lot, a child of his was delivered to the dragon. And any child was sacrificed who was not yet fifteen years of age.

The Princess Cleodolinda was aged fourteen. Every day her eyes were dim with tears for the child who was that day sacrificed. But her father, the King, never wept. His eyes were dry and his face pale. For his heart contained but one fear - that Cleodolinda would be chosen.

Then came the fateful day when the lot fell upon the Princess Cleodolinda, and she must be delivered to the dragon. The King mourned for her as she was placed outside the city wall to await the coming of the beast.

III

Now she had been standing thus but a short time, when she heard upon the ground the noise of a horse's hoofs and looked up to see who it was that approached so near to the city of Selene. And, having looked, her heart was filled with fear, for she beheld a knight of a fairer presence than any she had seen and of a wondrous gentleness; and she perceived that he knew not of the dragon.

This knight was a soldier of the Emperor Diocletian, St. George by name, one who had risen to high honor in the army and who was passing through Libya to join his men. When he perceived the Princess, standing pale and trembling outside the walls of the city, he paused on his way to ask what was her distress.

But the Princess, in a great agitation, replied, "Ah, sir, do not wait to question me, but press on thy way! For know, in yon marshes lurks a fearful dragon who has been the death of many a noble knight. Press on, I beseech thee, ere it issue from its lair."

But the knight replied, "I cannot press on and leave thee unprotected against the dragon."

And at that moment the dragon bestirred itself and began to crawl from its hiding-place.

"Alas," cried Cleodolinda, "the dragon is upon us! I beseech thee, Sir Knight, leave me before it be too late!"

But the knight, turning him about, bade her remain where she was and went out to meet the dragon.

When it observed him approach, the beast was struck with amazement, and, having paused for but a moment, it ran toward the knight with a great swiftness and beat its dark wings upon the ground as it ran.

When it drew near to him, it puffed out from its nostrils a smoke so dense that the knight was enveloped in it as in a cloud and darted hot flames from its eyes. Rearing its horrid body, it beat against the knight, dealing him fearful blows; but he, bending, thrust his spear against it and caught the blows upon his shield.

And having cast all his strength into it, he dealt the dragon a deadly thrust; but the spear glanced aside, for the scales of the beast were like steel plates and withstood the blow. Then the dragon, infuriated by the thrust, lashed itself against the knight and his horse and threw out a vapor deadlier than before and cast lightnings upon him from its eyes. And it writhed, an evil thing, about him, so that one would have said he must have been crushed; and wherever he thrust at it, that part was as if it had been clad in mail.

The fight lasted a long time, and the knight grew weary, though he fought with as great an ardor as at first. Through the deadly fumes that issued from the dragon the Princess could see his face shine out, and she saw that it was pale, yet lighted up by some radiance that shone from within. As he thrust at the dragon, this radiance grew greater, so that at last it was like the light of the sun.

But the dragon looped itself about the knight, and its poison was heavy upon him, so that to breathe was almost more pain than he could bear. Then he perceived that, no matter how the dragon writhed, it sought always to protect one place in its body--that place which lay beneath its left wing. And, nerving himself for a great blow, the knight bent himself downward and thrust his spear with a turn into that place.

So great was the strength required for the thrust that the knight left the spear in the wound for weariness, and as he raised himself he felt the dragon's clasp upon him loosen. Then the smoke ceased to belch from its nostrils, and the great beast fell to the ground.

Perceiving that the dragon was now helpless, though not dead, the knight called joyfully to the Princess; and he bade her that she should loosen her girdle and give it to him. When this was done, the knight bound it about the neck of the dragon and gave the girdle-ends into the hand of the Princess that she might lead the dragon toward the city.

Thereafter, when they had reached the city gates, these were opened to them with great joy by the people of Selene, who had watched from the city this great fight; and all were astonished to behold the loathsome dragon so guided by the Princess.

With his sword, and in the presence of all people, the knight despatched the dragon; and when this was done, he would have gone on his way.

But the King said, "What shall be given to this brave knight who hath so rid us of our enemy and hath restored to us the Princess Cleodolinda and saved our children?"

And the people cried of honors and wealth that should be given to the knight.

But he, when all had finished, thus replied, "I desire only that ye believe in the God who strengthened my hand to gain this victory and be baptized."

And when he had baptized the city into the Christian faith, he went on his way.

St. George and the Dragon   Name: _____

I. Vocabulary: Underline the following words in the legend. Define each word and use it in a short sentence below.

○ lustrous: _____
○ emanated: _____
○ agitation: _____
○ enveloped: _____
○ ardor: _____

II. Plot: Write a simple sentence or phrase to describe the main actions that take place in each scene.

Loathsome Bird	Bitter Weeping	Believe in God
1. _____	1. _____	1. _____
2. _____	2. _____	2. _____
3. _____	3. _____	3. _____

III. Characters: List and briefly describe the main characters in this legend.

_____
_____
_____

IV. Rewrite this legend. Be sure to:

○ Include and underline all of the vocabulary words.
○ Write at least three separate paragraphs.
○ Include the following additional requirements.

○
○

_____

○

The Miracle of the Sword in the Stone - Part 1

I

Now, when Uther Pendragon had passed through all the land, he came to London and ministered justice there. And it befell at a certain great banquet and high feast which the king made at Easter time, there came, with many other earls and barons, Gorlois, Duke of Cornwall, and his wife Igerna, who was the most famous beauty in all Britain. Soon thereafter, Gorlois being slain in battle, Uther determined to make Igerna his own wife. But in order to do this he sent for Merlin to ask for his help. This, therefore, Merlin promised him on one condition - namely that the king should give up the first son born of the marriage. For Merlin foreknew that this firstborn should be the long wished for prince, King Arthur.

When Uther, therefore, was at length happily wedded and his wife had delivered a son he commanded two knights and two ladies to take the child bound in rich cloth of gold and "deliver him to what poor man you meet at the postern gate of the castle." Thus the child was delivered to Merlin, who took the guise of a poor man, and was carried by him to a priest and christened by the name of Arthur. Then was he taken to the house of a bold and faithful knight named Sir Ector and was treated as his own son. There he remained for many years, no man ever knowing were he was save Merlin and the king.

In the hall of his Roman palace at London, King Uther, Pendragon of the Island of Britain, lay dying. He had been long sick with a wasting disease and forced to lie in his bed, gnawing his beard with wrath at his weakness, while the pagan Saxons ravened up and down the fair broad lands, leaving in their tracks the smoking ruin of broken towns and desolated villages where mothers lay dead beside their children on the hearths, fair churches stood pillaged and desecrated, and priests and nuns wandered in the wilds.

At length, when the pagans, bold and insolent, had ventured-near London, the king had been able to bear his shame and anguish no longer. He had put himself, in a litter, at the head of his army, and, meeting the fierce, brave pagans at Verulam (now called St. Albans), he had in a battle day-long and stubborn, forced them at length to fly with heavy slaughter.

Anon the king slept and lay thus for three further days, neither speaking nor moving. Many great lords and barons came craving to speak with Merlin, asking if the king were not better. But, looking into their crafty eyes and seeing there the pride and ambitions of their hearts, Merlin knew that they wished the king were already dead; for all thought that King Uther had no son to take the kingdom after him, and each great baron, strong in men, plotted to win the overlordship when the king should be gone.

"If he dieth and sayeth not which he shall name to succeed him," some asked, "say, Merlin, what's to be done?"

"I shall tell you," said Merlin. " Come ye all into this chamber to-morrow's morn, and, if God so wills, I will make the king speak."

II

Next morn, therefore, came all the great barons and lords into the high hall of the palace, and many were the proud and haughty glances passing among them.

Now, when all these were assembled about the bed of Uther, Merlin went to the side of the sleeping king and looked long and earnestly upon his closed eyes. Anon he passed his hands above the face of the king, and Uther instantly awoke and looked about him as if startled.

"Lord," said Merlin, " God's hand is drawing you to Him, and these your lords desire you to name your successor ere you pass from life. Is it not your desire that your son Arthur shall take the kingdom after you with your blessing?"

Those who craned towards the bed started and looked darkly at Merlin and then at each other; for none had heard of the son whom the wizard named Arthur. Then in the deep silence the dying king raised his hand in the sign of blessing, and in a hollow whisper said,

"Such is my desire. With God's blessing I wish my son Arthur to take this kingdom after me, and all that love me must follow him."

His eyes closed, a shiver passed down the tall frame as it lay beneath the clothes, and with a sigh the soul of Uther sped.

In a few days the king was buried in all solemnity with the dead of his kindred in the Roman temple that had been made a church, where now stands St. Paul's. Thereafter men waited and wondered, for the land was without a king, and none knew who was rightfully heir to the throne. Nevertheless, some were already wagering which of the great lords would conquer the others and take to himself the crown of Britain and the title of Pendragon.

As it neared the feast of Christmas, men heard that the Archbishop of London, who was then chief ruler of the Church, had been advised by Merlin and had sent letters to each and all the great nobles, bidding them come to a great council to be held at the church of St. Paul at Christmas. Now when men heard that this was done by the advice of Merlin, faces lightened and looked more joyful.

"Now shall things go right," said they, " for the old, old Merlin hath the deepest wisdom of all the earth."

On Christmas Eve the city throbbed with the clank of arms and the tramp of the great retinues of princes, kings, and powerful lords who had come at the arch-bishop's summons, and by day and night the narrow ways were crowded with armed men. Long ere the dawn of Christmas Day, the lords and the common people betook themselves along the wide road which led across to the church, which then stood in a wide space amid fields, and all knelt therein to mass.

While it was yet dark a great strange cry rang out in the churchyard. Some ran forth, and there by the wall behind the high altar they saw a vast stone, four-square, that had not been there before, and in the middle of it was stuck a rich sword. On the blade were written words in Latin, which a clerk read forth, which said, "Whoso pulleth this sword out of this stone is the rightful King of all Britain."

The clerk ran into the church and told the archbishop, and men were all amazed and would have gone instantly to see this marvel, but the archbishop bade them stay.

"Finish your prayers to God," he said, " for no man may touch this strange thing till high mass be done."

When mass was finished, all poured forth from the church and thronged about the stone and marveled at the words on the sword. All present tried to pull out the sword, but by none was it moved a jot, and all stood about discomfited, looking with black looks at one another and the stone.

III

"He that is rightwise born ruler of Britain is not here," said the archbishop at length, " but doubt not he shall come in God's good time."

So ten knights were chosen to watch and keep the sword and there was a proclamation made through the land that whosoever wanted could try to pull the sword from the stone. But though great multitudes of people came, both gentle and simple, no man could ever move the sword a hair's breadth from its place.

Now, at New Year's Eve a great tournament was to be held in London, which the archbishop had devised to keep together the lords and commons, lest they should grow estranged in the troublous and unsettled times.

To this tournament there came, with many other knights, Sir Ector. With him rode his son, Sir Kay, but recently made knight, to take his part in the jousting, and young Arthur also to witness all the sports and fighting. As they rode toward the jousts, Sir Kay found suddenly that he had left his sword at home.

"Do you ride back, young Arthur," said Kay, "and fetch me my sword, for if I do not have it I may not fight."

Willingly Arthur turned his horse and rode back swiftly. But when he had arrived at the house he found it shut up and none was within, for all had gone to the jousts. As he looked and saw the tower of St. Paul's church through the trees, he bethought him of the sword in the stone, about which many men had spoken in his hearing.

"I will ride thither," said he, " and see if I may get that sword for my brother, for he shall not be without a sword this day."

When he came to the churchyard, he tied his horse to the stile and went to the tent wherein was the sword. He found the place un-watched, and the flashing sword was sticking by the point in the stone.

Lightly he grasped the handle of the sword with one hand, and it came forth straightway!

Then, glad that his brother should not be without a sword, he swiftly got upon his horse and rode on and delivered the sword to Sir Kay and thought no more of aught but the splendid knights that were at the jousts.

The Miracle of the Sword in the Stone – Part 1

Name: _____

I. Vocabulary: Underline the following words in the legend. Define each word and use it in a short sentence below.

○ pillaged: _____

○ anon: _____

○ solemnity: _____

○ retinues: _____

○ discomfited: _____

II. Plot: Write a simple sentence or phrase to describe the main actions that take place in each scene.

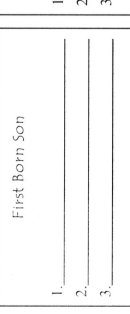

First Born Son

1. _____
2. _____
3. _____

Black Looks

1. _____
2. _____
3. _____

With One Hand

1. _____
2. _____
3. _____

III. Characters: List and briefly describe the main characters in this legend.

_____

_____

_____

IV. Rewrite this legend. Be sure to:

○ Include and underline all of the vocabulary words.

○ Write at least three separate paragraphs.

○ Include the following additional requirements.

_____

_____

_____

59

The Miracle of the Sword in the Stone - Part 2

I

When Arthur had given Kay the sword he looked at it, and the writing, and knew it was the sword of the stone and marveled how young Arthur had possessed himself thereof; and being of a covetous and sour mind he thought how he might make advantage for himself. He went to his father, Sir Ector, and said: "Lo, father, this is the sword of the stone, and surely am I rightful king."

Sir Ector knew the sword and marveled, but his look was stern as he gazed into the crafty eyes of his son.

"Come ye with me," he said, and all three rode to the church and alit from their horses and went in.

Sir Ector strode up to the altar and, turning to his son, said sternly: "Now, swear on God's book and the holy relics how thou didst get this sword."

Sir Kay's heart went weak, and he stammered but did not reply.

"How gat you this sword?" asked Sir Ector of Kay.

"Sir, I will tell you," said Arthur and so told him all as it had happened.

Sir Ector marveled what this should mean, for Arthur had been given to him to nourish and rear by Merlin, but the wizard had only told him that the babe was a son of a dead lady, whose lord had been slain by the pagans.

Then Sir Ector went to the stone and bade Arthur put back the sword into the stone, which the young man did easily.

Thereupon Sir Ector strove with all his strength to draw the sword forth again, but though he pulled till he sweated, he could not stir the sword.

"Now you essay it," he said to his son. But naught that Sir Kay could do availed.

"Now do you try," he bade Arthur.

Arthur lightly grasped the handle with one hand, and the sword came out without hindrance.

Therewith Sir Ector sank to his knees, and Sir Kay also. And they bared their heads and did homage to Arthur.

"Alas," said Arthur, "my own dear father and brother, why kneel ye so to me?"

"Nay, nay, my lord Arthur, it is not so," said Sir Ector, "for I was never your father. I wot well ye are of higher blood than I weened. For Merlin delivered you to me while yet ye were a babe."

When young Arthur heard this he fell upon Sir Ector's neck and wept and made great lamentation, "For now," said he, "I have in one day lost my father and my mother and my brother."

II

Then hastily Sir Ector rode to the archbishop and told him how and by whom the sword had been achieved from the stone. Thereupon the archbishop called a great meeting on Twelfth Day of all the kings and barons.

On the day appointed, all men gathered in the churchyard of St. Paul's. From day dawn to the evening the kings and princes and lords strove each in his turn to draw the sword from the stone. But none of them availed to move it. While they stood about, dark of look, gnawing their lips with rage and disappointment, the archbishop turned privily to Sir Ector and bade him bring Arthur.

The young man came, quietly clad in a tunic of brown samite, of medium height, with curly hair above a fair face of noble though mild mien. As he came among the richly clad nobles, they looked haughtily at him and wondered who he was and why he came, for as yet none had been told that the sword had been drawn by him.

The archbishop, tall, white-haired and reverend, called Arthur to him and said in grave tones, "My son, I have heard a strange tale of thee, and whether it be true or false, God shall decide. Now, therefore, do ye take hold upon this sword and essay to draw it from the stone."

The proud barons, some with looks amazed and others with sneering laughter, pressed about the young man as he stepped towards the stone. Arthur took the handle of the sword with his right hand, and the sword seemed to fall into his grasp.

Then befell great confusion and dispute, for some cried out that it was the will of Heaven and "Long live King Arthur," but many more were full of wrath and said, "What! Would you give the ancient sceptre of this land unto an unknown boy?" And the contention grew greatly till the archbishop spoke.

"Peace, lords!" he said, calmly meeting the raging looks about him. "Ye know what words are about the sword, and this youth hath drawn the sword. I know naught of tricks or wizardry, but I think high Heaven hath chosen this way of showing who shall be lord of this land, and I think this young man is the rightful king of us all. We will have the sword put back and set a watch over it," he declared, "and we will meet here again at Candlemas

60

and essay the sword. And at that time we will try the sword once more."

So was it agreed by all, and ten knights watched day and night about the stone and the sword.

But it befell at Candlemas as it had befallen at Twelfth Day, that for all their strength and might, none of the kings or barons could draw forth the sword; but into the hand of the unknown Arthur the weapon seemed to fall. Whereat they were all sore aggrieved and rageful and resolved that they would have yet another trial at Easter. It befell at the feast of Easter as it had befallen before, and this time the kings and lords for angry spite would have fallen upon Arthur and slain him, but the archbishop threatened them with the most dreadful ban of Holy Church. They forbore, therefore, and went aside and declared that it was their will to essay the sword again at the high feast of Pentecost.

By Merlin's advice the young Arthur went never about, unless the five friends of Uther were with him, that is to say, Sir Ector and his son Sir Kay, Sir Bedevere, Sir Baudwin, and Sir Ulfius. And though at divers times men were found skulking or hiding in the horse-stall, the dark wood by the hall, or the bend in the lane, in places where Arthur might pass, no harm came to him by reason of the loving watch of those noble knights.

Again at the feast of Pentecost men gathered in the churchyard of St. Paul's, and the press of people was such that no man had ever seen the like. Once more the kings and princes and great barons, to the number of forty-nine, came forward, and each in turn pulled and drew at the sword in the stone until the sweat stood on their brows. Nevertheless, though the sword point was but the width of a palm in the stone, not the mightiest of them could move it by the breadth of a hair.

Then a cry came from among the common people, and so strong was it that the nobles looked as if they hated to hear it. "Let Arthur draw the sword!" was the call from a thousand throats.

III

The venerable archbishop came and took Arthur by the hand and led him towards the sword. Again the young man held the rich pommel with his single hand, and, that which none of the forty-nine great men could do, he did as easily as if he but plucked a flower.

A fierce cry leaped from among the thousands of the common people.

"Arthur shall be our king!" they cried. "Long live king Arthur! We will no longer deny him!"

Many of the princes and barons cried out with the commons that this was their will also; but eleven of the most powerful and ambitious showed by their arrogant and angry gestures that they refused to own Arthur as their lord.

For a long time the uproar raged, the cries of the common folk becoming fiercer and more menacing against the counter cries of the eleven kings and their adherents.

At length from among the people there came the governor of London who, in his rich robes of office, leaped upon the stone where but lately the sword had been.

"My lords, I speak the will of the commons," he cried, and at his voice all were silent. "We have taken counsel together, and we will have Arthur for our king. We will put him no more in delay, for we all see that it is God's will that he shall be our king, and who that holdeth against him, we will slay."

With that he got down from the stone, kneeled before Arthur, put the keys of the city in his hands, and rendered homage unto him. The great multitude kneeled likewise, bowing their bare heads, and cried him mercy because they had denied him so long.

Because they feared the great multitude, the eleven kings kneeled with them, but in their hearts there was rage and rebellion.

Then Arthur took the sword between his hands, and, going into the church, he laid it on the high altar, and the archbishop blessed him. Then, since Arthur was as yet unknighted, King Kador of Cornwall, who was brother of King Uther, made him a knight. Standing up in the sight of all the people, lords and commons, Arthur laid his left hand upon the holy relics; then, lifting up his right hand, he swore that he would be a true king, to stand forth as their ruler in justice and mercy, to keep them from oppression, to redress their wrongs, and to establish right throughout the length and breadth of his dominions.

Men went forth from the church in great joy, for now they had a king they loved, and they felt that the land was safe from civil strife and the griefs of war.

The Miracle of the Sword in the Stone – Part 2

Name: _____

I. Vocabulary: Underline the following words in the legend. Define each word and use it in a short sentence below.

○ essay: _____

○ lamentation: _____

○ mien: _____

○ menacing: _____

○ redress: _____

II. Plot: Write a simple sentence or phrase to describe the main actions that take place in each scene.

On God's Book	Holidays	The True King
1. _____	1. _____	1. _____
2. _____	2. _____	2. _____
3. _____	3. _____	3. _____

III. Characters: List and briefly describe the main characters in this legend.

_____

_____

_____

IV. Rewrite this legend. Be sure to:

○ Include and underline all of the vocabulary words.

○ Write at least three separate paragraphs.

○ Include the following additional requirements.

○ _____

○ _____

○ _____

The Sword Excalibur

I

After Arthur was knighted, a coronation feast was held. Now there were still eleven kings whose hearts were filled with rage that a boy of unknown birth was to become king of Britain. And these met together and went up to the coronation feast as if to do him homage; and there they ate and drank such things as were set before them at the royal banquet, sitting with the others in the great hall.

But when after the banquet Arthur began, according to the ancient royal custom, to bestow great boons and fiefs on whom he would, they all with one accord rose up and scornfully refused his gifts, crying that they would take nothing from a beardless boy of low or unknown birth but would instead give him good gifts of hard sword-strokes between the neck and shoulders.

At this a deadly tumult arose in the hall and every man there was ready to fight. But Arthur leaped up as a flame of fire against them, and all his knights and barons drawing their swords, rushed after him upon them and began a full sore battle; and presently the king's party prevailed and drove the rebels from the hall and from the city, closing the gates behind them; and King Arthur broke his sword upon them in this eagerness and rage.

But amongst them were six kings of great renown and might who more than all raged against Arthur and determined to destroy him, namely, King Lot, King Nanters, King Urien, King Carados, King Yder, and King Anguisant. These six, therefore, joining their armies together, laid close siege to the city of Caerleon, wherefrom King Arthur had so shamefully driven them.

And after fifteen days Merlin came suddenly into their camp and asked them what this treason meant. Then he declared to them that Arthur was no base adventurer, but King Uther's son, whom they were bound to serve and honor. Some of the Kings, when they heard Merlin speak marveled and believed him; but others, as King Lot, laughed him and his words to scorn and mocked him for a conjurer and wizard. But it was agreed that Arthur should come forth and speak with the kings.

So Arthur went forth to them at the city gate and spared them not in his speech but spoke to them as king and chieftain, telling them plainly that he would make them all bow to him if he lived, unless they chose to do him homage there and then. This they refused and when his speech had ended they parted in great wrath, and each side armed in haste.

Then Arthur called for Merlin and said to him, "I have need of a sword with which to chastise these rebels."

"Come with me then," said Merlin, "for close by there is a sword that I can get for thee."

II

So they secretly rode out that night till they came to a fair and broad lake, and in the midst of it King Arthur saw an arm thrust up, clothed in white samite, and holding a great sword in the hand.

"Lo! Yonder is the sword I spoke of," said Merlin.

Then they saw a damsel floating on the lake in the moonlight. "What damsel is that?" asked the king.

"That is the lady of the lake," replied Merlin; "and she will come to you anon, and then speak courteously to her and she will give you the sword when you ask."

Therewith the damsel came to King Arthur and saluted him, and he saluted her and said, "Lady, what sword is that, that yonder arm holdeth above the water? I would that it were mine, for I have no sword."

"Sir King," said the lady of the lake, "that sword is mine, and if thou wilt give me in return a gift whenever I shall ask it of thee, thou shalt have it."

"By my faith," said he, "I will give thee any gift that thou shalt ask."

"Well," said the damsel, "go into yonder barge and row thyself unto the sword and take it and the scabbard with thee, and I will ask my gift of thee when I see my time."

So King Arthur and Merlin alighted and tied their horses to two trees, and King Arthur went into the barge; and when he came to the sword that the hand held, King Arthur took it by the handle and bore it with him, and the arm and the hand went down under the water; and so he came back to land, and with Merlin rode again to Caerleon.

III

On the morrow Merlin bade King Arthur to set fiercely on the enemy; and in the meanwhile three hundred good knights went over to King Arthur from the rebels' side. Then at the spring of day, when they had scarce left their tents, he fell on them with might and main, and Sir Badewaine, Sir Kay, and Sir Brastias slew in the right hand and on the left marvelously; and ever in the thickest of the fight King Arthur raged like a young lion and laid on with his sword and did wondrous deeds of arms to the joy and admiration of the knights and barons who beheld him.

Then King Lot, King Carados, and the King of the Hundred Knights-who also was with them-going round to the rear, set on King Arthur fiercely from behind; but Arthur, turning to his knights, fought ever in the foremost press until his horse was slain beneath him. At that, King Lot rode furiously at him and smote him down; but rising straightway and being set again on horseback, he drew his sword Excalibur that he had gained from the lady of the lake, which, shining brightly as the light of thirty torches, dazzled the eyes of his enemies. And therewith falling on them afresh with all his knights, he drove them back and slew them in great numbers, and Merlin by his arts scattered among them fire and pitchy smoke, so that they broke and fled. Then all the common people of Caerleon, seeing them give way, rose up with one accord and rushed at them with clubs and staves and chased them far and wide and slew many great knights and lords, and the remainder of them fled and were seen no more. Thus King Arthur won his first battle and put his enemies to shame.

The Sword Excalibur

Name: _____

I. Vocabulary: Underline the following words in the legend. Define each word and use it in a short sentence below.

○ coronation: _____

○ homage: _____

○ fiefs: _____

○ chastise: _____

○ samite: _____

II. Plot: Write a simple sentence or phrase to describe the main actions that take place in each scene.

Coronation Feast	Excalibur	Thirty Torches
1. _____	1. _____	1. _____
2. _____	2. _____	2. _____
3. _____	3. _____	3. _____

III. Characters: List and briefly describe the main characters in this legend.

_____

_____

_____

IV. Rewrite this legend. Be sure to:

○ Include and underline all of the vocabulary words.

○ Write at least three separate paragraphs.

○ Include the following additional requirements.

_____

_____

_____

SIR GAWAIN'S MARRIAGE

I

Once upon a time King Arthur held his court in merry Carlisle, when a damsel came before him and craved a boon. It was for vengeance upon a caitiff knight who had made her lover captive and despoiled her of her lands. King Arthur commanded to bring him his sword, Excalibur, and to saddle his steed and rode forth without delay to right the lady's wrong. Ere long he reached the castle of the grim baron and challenged him to the conflict. But the castle stood on magic ground, and the spell was such that no knight could tread thereon but straight his courage fell and his strength decayed. King Arthur felt the charm, and before a blow was struck his sturdy limbs lost their strength, and his head grew faint. He was fain to yield himself prisoner to the churlish knight who refused to release him except upon condition that he should return at the end of a year and bring a true answer to the question, "What thing is it which women most desire?" or in default thereof surrender himself and his lands. King Arthur accepted the terms and gave his oath to return at the time appointed. During the year the king rode east and he rode west and he inquired of all whom he met what thing it is which all women most desire. Some told him riches, some pomp and state, some mirth, some flattery, and some a gallant knight. But in the diversity of answers he could find no sure dependence.

II

The year was well nigh spent when, one day, as he rode thoughtfully through a forest, he saw sitting beneath a tree a lady of such hideous aspect that he turned away his eyes, and when she greeted him in seemly sort made no answer. "What wight art thou," the lady said, "that will not speak to me? It may chance that I may resolve thy doubts, though I be not fair of aspect." "If thou wilt do so," said King Arthur, "choose what reward thou wilt, thou grim lady, and it shall be given thee." "Swear me this upon thy faith," she said, and Arthur swore it. Then the lady told him the secret and demanded her reward which was that the king should find some fair and courtly knight to be her husband.

King Arthur hastened to the grim baron's castle and told him one by one all the answers which he had received from his various advisers, except the last, and not one was admitted as the true one. "Now yield thee, Arthur," the giant said, "for thou hast not paid thy ransom, and thou and thy lands are forfeited to me." Then King Arthur said:

"Yet hold thy hand, thou proud baron,
I pray thee hold thy hand.
And give me leave to speak once more,
In rescue of my land.
This morn, as I came over a moor,
I saw a lady set,
Between an oak and a green holly,
All clad in red scarlet.
She says all women would have their will,
This is their chief desire;
Now yield, as thou art a baron true,
That I have paid my hire."

"It was my sister that told thee this," the churlish baron exclaimed. "Vengeance light on her! I will some time or other do her as ill a turn."

King Arthur rode homeward, but not light of heart; for he remembered the promise he was under to the loathly lady to give her one of his young and gallant knights for a husband. He told his grief to Sir Gawain, his nephew, and he replied, "Be not sad, my lord, for I will marry the loathly lady." King Arthur replied:

"Now nay, now nay, good Sir Gawaine,
My sister's son ye be;
The loathly lady's all too grim,
And all too foule for thee."

But Gawain persisted, and the king at last, with sorrow of heart, consented that Gawain should be his ransom. So, one day, the king and his knights rode to the forest, met the loathly lady, and brought her to the court. Sir Gawain stood the scoffs and jeers of his companions as he best might, and the marriage was solemnized, but not with the usual festivities.

III

When night came and they were alone together, Sir Gawain could not conceal his aversion; and the lady asked him why he sighed so heavily and turned away his face. He candidly confessed it was on account of three things, her age, her ugliness, and her low degree. The lady, not at all offended, replied with excellent arguments to all his objections. She showed him that with age is discretion, with ugliness security from rivals, and that all true gentility depends, not upon the accident of birth, but upon the character of the individual.

Sir Gawain made no reply; but, turning his eyes on his bride, what was his amazement to perceive that she wore no longer the unseemly aspect that had so distressed him. She then told him that the form she had worn was not her true form but a disguise imposed upon her by a wicked enchanter and that she was condemned to wear it until two things should happen; one, that she should obtain some young and gallant knight to be her husband. This having been done, one half of the charm was removed. She was now at liberty to wear her true form for half the time, and she bade him choose whether he would have her fair by day and ugly by night or the reverse. Sir Gawain would fain have had her look her best by night, when he alone should see her and show her repulsive visage, if at all, to others. But she reminded him how much more pleasant it would be to her to wear her best looks in the throng of knights and ladies by day. Sir Gawain yielded and gave up his will to hers. This alone was wanting to dissolve the charm. The lovely lady now with joy assured him that she should change no more; but as she now was so would she remain by night as well as by day.

The dissolution of the charm which had held the lady also released her brother, the "grim baron," for he too had been implicated in it. He ceased to be a churlish oppressor and became a gallant and generous knight as any at Arthur's court.

Sir Gawain's Marriage

Name: _____

I. Vocabulary: Underline the following words in the legend. Define each word and use it in a short sentence below.

○ boon: _____

○ churlish: _____

○ ransom: _____

○ solemnized: _____

○ aversion: _____

II. Plot: Write a simple sentence or phrase to describe the main actions that take place in each scene.

What Women Desire
1. _____
2. _____
3. _____

Loathly Lady
1. _____
2. _____
3. _____

Double Charm
1. _____
2. _____
3. _____

III. Characters: List and briefly describe the main characters in this legend.

_____

_____

_____

IV. Rewrite this legend. Be sure to:

○ Include and underline all of the vocabulary words.

○ Write at least three separate paragraphs.

○ Include the following additional requirements.

Beaumains, the Knight of the Kitchen - Part 1

I

King Arthur had gone with his knights of the Round Table to Kin-Kenadon, which is upon the sand near Wales, to keep the great feast of Pentecost. In the high hall the tables were set for dinner, and the floor was freshly strewn with rushes, flowers, and fennel, so that the place smelled as sweet as a field. The cook and his scullions came to and fro through the door of the kitchen but as yet King Arthur would not sit to dinner. For it was his custom never to go to meat on Pentecost until he had heard or seen some great marvel or adventure.

Then Sir Gawain looked out of the castle window, and he beheld three men on horseback who came rapidly toward the castle and behind them a dwarf who ran on foot. Suddenly Gawain laughed and turned to the King to say, "My lord, wait no longer for thy dinner, for here cometh adventure toward thee, hard and fast."

And even as the king took his seat on the high dais in the hall and his knights sat at the Round Table, there came into the hall these three men whom Sir Gawain had seen. Now two of them were exceedingly tall, but the third was taller still; and as he came he leant upon the shoulders of the other men, for he walked between them, as if he could not walk alone. Yet was he strong of frame and of a healthy color, and he bore no wounds.

When he had come to that place where King Arthur sat, the young man raised himself with ease, and it was seen that he was a foot and a half taller than those beside him. And he spoke to the King, saying: "Sir, here have I come to ask of thee the granting of three gifts; but of these I will ask but one on this occasion, and the other two on Pentecost a year hence."

II

Now King Arthur, looking upon the young man, found him straight and fair and manly; and, although he knew nothing of him, he liked him right well. He said, "Ask, my son, and thy petition shall be granted thee."

"Sir," said the stranger, "the gift I ask is this, that for twelve months thou wilt provide me with meat and drink."

"Nay," said the King, "call not my hospitality a gift. Is it not the due of any man who hath need of it? Eat and drink what thou wilt but require of me that which shall be more worthy of thee, for I believe thy blood to be noble."

"Of that I can tell thee nothing," said the young man; "neither do I ask aught but hospitality till these twelve months be past."

Then the King, who was ever generous, called Sir Kay, who was steward, and bade him that he should give the young man such sustenance as he needed day by day for one year as if he were a lord's son. "For," said Arthur, "I trow he is of gentle blood."

But Sir Kay was wroth and scornful and cared not for the task with which the King had charged him. "This lout hath no gentle blood," said he, "or he would have asked for a horse and harness, as becomes a knight, that he might do noble deeds. Nay, he is some low fellow who would sup from a full dish. For as his petition is, so is he. Today I give him a name that will serve him well. He shall be called Beaumains, that is to say, fair hands, for his hands are large and fair, and I warrant he plies them diligently when he sups from the King's bowl!"

At this speech two knights were exceedingly wroth; and these were that valiant knight Sir Launcelot and Sir Gawain, who was son to the King's sister. These bade Sir Kay that he should cease his mocking, for which he would surely repent, since they believed the stranger would prove one day a knight most noble.

"Nay," said Sir Kay, "On my life I would swear he is only some lazy fellow from an abbey where food hath failed, and so he has come hither for sustenance. He shall be a kitchen knight, for there his place is. I shall feed him in the kitchen till he be as broad as he is long."

So Kay sat down to his meat laughing; and the two men and the dwarf who had accompanied the young man having left him, Beaumains went to the hall door, sitting among the boys and serving men and sharing their fare. And at night he slept with the youths of the kitchen, for so Sir Kay would have it. And in the daytime he supped with them again.

Then Sir Launcelot and Sir Gawain were angry again; but Sir Kay took no heed of their speech. And they would have had it that Beaumains should have meat and drink and lodging from them, but the young man would accept nothing but in all things he would have himself treated as Sir Kay ordered, and with meekness he bore that knight's ungentle words.

Thus he lived in the kitchen, eating broken scraps and lying at night where the scullions lay, except that he was given the chilliest spot furthest from the fire. But he did what he was bidden to do with a cheerful air and was ever willing to work. And if there was any jousting of knights or any other sights of prowess, these would he see with the greatest delight. In any sports or trials of strength or skill among the serving-men, he was ever foremost, and none could overcome him in wrestling or at quarterstaff, nor could any throw the bar or cast the stone so far as he could, no, not by two yards.

III

Now twelve months were well past, and again King Arthur kept the great feast of Pentecost; and, as before, he would not sit down to meat till news of some adventure came to him. As he waited there came into the hall a damsel, one of a proud mien, but with a smile that was wondrous sweet--though in truth she could be moved to smile but seldom--and saluting the King, she asked him for a knight who would succour a lady in distress.

"Who is this lady?" asked the King. "And from what distress doth she suffer?"

"Nay," said the damsel, "what her name is I may not divulge to thee; but she is of noble blood, and owns wide lands. Her trouble is that she is besieged by a tyrannous knight, so that she may not leave her own castle. And the knight that besieges her is known as the Knight of the Reed Lands."

"I know nothing of him," replied King Arthur.

But Sir Gawain said, "I know more of him than I well care to know. For I once escaped from him, and that with great difficulty. He hath, it is said, the strength of seven men."

"Fair lady," said the King, "I doubt not that many a knight here would ride with gladness to the succor of thy lady; but because thou wilt neither state her name nor where she dwelleth, I am loth to let any knight go."

"Then I must fare farther," said the damsel. And she would have withdrawn herself.

Then from the crowd of scullions and kitchen lads that hung about the serving-tables came Beaumains, his dress smirched, but his handsome face lit up and his eyes burning with eagerness.

"Sir king!" he cried, holding up his hand, " a boon I crave!"

As he came to the step of the dais the damsel shrank from him is if he had been something foul.

"Say on," replied the king to the young man.

"God thank you, my king," went on Beaumains. "I have been these twelve months in your kitchen and have had my full living, as ye did graciously order, and now I ask for the two further gifts ye promised."

"Ye have but to ask," replied the king.

"Sir, they are these," said Beaumains. "First, that ye will grant me this adventure of the damsel."

"I grant it you," said King Arthur.

"Then, sir, this is the other - that ye shall bid Sir Lancelot du Lake to follow me and to make me a knight when the time arrives."

Then replied the King, "My son, I grant thee thy requests."

But the lady was exceedingly wroth, and her eyes flashed with scorn as she turned to the king: "Shame on thee!" she cried; "will you give me a kitchen scullion to aid me?"

With that she hastened from the hall, mounted her horse, and rode away. But Beaumains heeded not her anger. And one came to him telling him that a dwarf had arrived bringing him his horse and armor. Therefore he went away to make himself ready for the adventure.

And when he was made ready, there was none that did not wonder at the richness of his gear; but he was without spear or shield.

Beaumains, Knight of the Kitchen – Part 1

Name:_____

I. Vocabulary: Underline the following words in the legend. Define each word and use it in a short sentence below.

○ Pentecost:_____

○ fennel:_____

○ dais:_____

○ scullions:_____

○ succor:_____

II. Plot: Write a simple sentence or phrase to describe the main actions that take place in each scene.

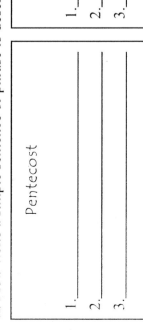

Pentecost	"Fair Hands"	Reed Lands
1.	1.	1.
2.	2.	2.
3.	3.	3.

III. Characters: List and briefly describe the main characters in this legend.

_____

_____

_____

IV. Rewrite this legend. Be sure to:

○ Include and underline all of the vocabulary words.

○ Write at least three separate paragraphs.

○ Include the following additional requirements.

Beaumains, the Knight of the Kitchen - Part 2

I

Then Beaumains took leave of King Arthur and of Sir Gawain and asked Sir Lancelot to follow him.

Many people went to the door of the hall to see Beaumains mount his horse and ride after the damsel, and the way he sat his steed, with its trappings of gold and purple, excited their admiration. But all wondered to see that Beaumains had neither shield nor spear, and some laughed and said, "The ignorant churl! Doth he think the mere sight of him on horseback will affright his enemies, that he carries neither shield nor lance?"

When Beaumains had ridden away with the damsel and with the dwarf following after, Sir Kay said, "I will pursue this kitchen-boy of mine and see if the fellow knows his master."

"Nay," said Sir Launcelot and Sir Gawaine, "leave the youth in peace. Thou hast already slighted him grievously and hast laid up for thyself future shame."

But Sir Kay heeded them not, and, getting upon his horse, he rode after Beaumains.

And when he was yet some distance behind him, he cried out to the youth to wait for him.

"It is I. Dost not thou know me, Beaumains?" cried he.

Then Beaumains drew in his horse and waited; and the damsel looked upon the youth scornfully. And when Sir Kay approached, Beaumains cried boldly, "Indeed I know thee well, for thou art a knight of little kindliness and hast ever used me ill."

At these words Sir Kay flew into a fury and rushed at him with his spear. But Beaumains, having no spear, gripped his sword and turned the blow aside and then another blow. Then leant Beaumains forward and thrust the knight through with his sword; and it was a neat thrust that he gave, and Sir Kay fell to the ground with a great wound.

Then Beaumains took the spear and shield of Sir Kay and had them for his own; and he bade the dwarf that he should mount Sir Kay's horse and go no more on foot. And he had but done this when he beheld Sir Launcelot, who was following him.

Then he proffered Sir Launcelot to joust with him, and immediately they flew together, the while the damsel looked on with a raised chin.

"I wonder at thee, Sir Launcelot, that thou shouldst joust with a kitchen knave!" cried she, mocking.

But neither Sir Launcelot nor Beaumains gave her heed, for they were thinking of a different matter. Great blows did the kitchen-boy deal, and much ado had Sir Launcelot to hold himself against them, for they were more like the blows of a giant than a man. At length they came upon the ground by reason of the force of their blows, and Sir Launcelot helped Beaumains to come clear of his horse, whereupon they fell upon each other with their swords.

And after they had fought till they were weary--and Sir Launcelot was almost overcome with the difficulty of defending himself from Beaumains, for the kitchen-boy fought with as great an ardor on foot as on his horse--Sir Launcelot cried, "Hold, Beaumains! have not we fought enough to show thy skill? Our quarrel is not so serious that we need fight further."

Said Beaumains, dropping his hand, "I have no quarrel with thee, Sir Launcelot, and I give thee thanks that thou didst not disdain to joust with me. Fain would I be knighted of thee ere I go farther upon my adventure; thinkest thou that I may prove a true knight?"

"Indeed I have little doubt of it!" said Sir Launcelot, "for I had difficulty with thee beyond what I have had in jousting with any champion."

II

And with that he made Beaumains knight with a right good-will; afterwards setting himself to see to Sir Kay and his hurt.

Sir Beaumains and his damsel rode on, and immediately she began to upbraid him, calling him the kitchen knight, and by other means making little of him. And ever she wondered that Sir Launcelot should have deigned to joust with him, and ever she mourned that Sir Kay should have been wounded by a knight so sorry.

But Sir Beaumains would not leave her, in spite of all her uncivil words, for he was determined to go upon this adventure.

And as they pressed on through the woods, there came running toward them as fast as he could a fellow whose garments were grievously torn, as if others had wrestled with him, and upon his face fear was written.

Then called Sir Beaumains to him, asking him what ailed him; and he replied how his lord had been set upon in the wood by six thieves and how he himself was fleeing from these plunderers who had maltreated him; but that they had bound his lord that he could not flee.

Sir Beaumains had no sooner heard this story, than he bade the fellow guide him to the spot where his master lay. And having reached it he fell furiously upon the thieves, slaying three of them and putting the other three to rout. Then he followed these three and slew them also, lest they should do mischief to other good knights.

And having carried this adventure to its end, he went with the rescued knight to his castle which was at no great distance; and there he and the damsel passed the night, proceeding the next morning upon their way.

Now they came upon a great forest, and when they had traversed but a part of it they found a river which had but one crossing. And this crossing two knights held, waiting on the other side.

"Come, wilt thou fight with those bold knights, kitchen knave?" asked the damsel, "or shall we return and go by another way?"

"I will not return," said Sir Beaumains; "and I think ill of thee that thou shouldst so question me."

Then, without further waste of words, he rode into the stream, and immediately one of the knights advanced to meet him.

Half-way across the stream they encountered, and there they fought valiantly; but Sir Beaumains gave the strange knight a blow upon the head that was too strong for him, and he was overcome and fell into the stream.

Then rode Sir Beaumains forward to meet that other knight, and, having encountered him, he slew him also. And when he had done this, he brought the damsel across the stream.

But she had no thanks for him. "Keep thee at a distance, kitchen knight," cried she, "for I like little the air of the kitchen which hangs about thee! Think not that I esteem thee more highly on account of thy deeds! For I know well that the first knight fell into the stream and was drowned because his foot caught upon a stone. As for the second, thou hadst wit to creep behind him, else hadst thou not slain him. Away from me! I like thee little by my side."

But Sir Beaumains moved from her not one inch. As for her bitter words, he rode on with an air as if he had not heard them. For this she liked him the less.

And after a time they came to a black country, and in the black country grew a black hawthorn, and on the black hawthorn hung a black shield, and by the shield was a black spear, and by the spear a great black horse, and a black stone was hard by the horse.

"Now are we in the lands of the Black Knight," said the damsel. "Fly, kitchen knight, while there be time, ere he catch sight of thee."

"Nay, it comes to me that I like better to ride forward," said Sir Beaumains; "for I have a fancy to see this Black Knight." And he cast her not a glance.

III

Then came the Black Knight riding toward them on a horse even blacker than the first they had seen and clad in black armor, and his eyes were as black as coals. And immediately the damsel began to make moan to him, as if in pity, that he would spare Sir Beaumains.

"For this is but a kitchen knave," said she, "whose head hath been turned through riding with a lady of my quality. I pray thee, Sir Knight, do him no ill."

Said the Black Knight, "He is not garbed as a kitchen knave, but as a knight."

"It is so he imagines himself," said she scornfully. "Nevertheless he is of King Arthur's kitchen, as I have said. Many knightly deeds hath he done, but all by misadventure, not by skill. For Chance hath this fellow in her care and ever favors him. And he hath killed good knights."

"Damsel," said the Black Knight, "I shall do him no evil. Bid him only that he leave with me his horse and armor, for I would have him wage no more mischief."

Then cried Sir Beaumains in a high voice, "Sir, thou talkest lightly of my horse and armor, but know that they are mine, not thine, and that I will not yield them. Yet will I pass through thy lands, and from them, and go upon my way."

At these words the Black Knight became wrathful, and he warned Sir Beaumains that he would fight with him. So they drew apart some distance and then rushed together; and with the force of the blow he gave the spear of the Black Knight broke. And at the same moment Sir Beaumains thrust his spear into the Black Knight's side, so that it brake also, and a part of it remained there.

Yet the Black Knight drew his sword and fought with that, and he wounded Sir Beaumains sorely ere he died from his wound.

Then Sir Beaumains, seeing the fineness of the Black Knight's armour, alighted and clad himself in it; and he took the Black Knight's horse also and mounted it. Then rode he after the damsel who had gone on ahead.

"Behold him! how pleased he is with himself!" cried she. "So thou hast slain the Black Knight, kitchen knave? Be not so high in the glance thou givest. He whom thou shalt meet, if thou followest out this quest, will be a worse knight to joust with than the Black Knight. Yet would I fain be rid of thee before then. I would not see thee discomfited, kitchen knave."

"Damsel," said Sir Beaumains, "whether I be a kitchen knave or not is not known to thee; but this thou mayest know, that I will not leave thee till this quest be done."

"Upon thine own head be it!" said the damsel; and Sir Beaumains thought she sighed. Then rode they on in silence.

Beaumains, the Knight of the Kitchen – Part 2

Name: _____

I. Vocabulary: Underline the following words in the legend. Define each word and use it in a short sentence below.

○ churl: _____
○ ardor: _____
○ deigned: _____
○ maltreated: _____
○ discomfited: _____

II. Plot: Write a simple sentence or phrase to describe the main actions that take place in each scene.

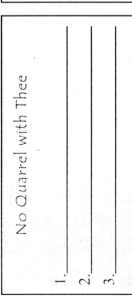

No Quarrel with Thee

1. _____
2. _____
3. _____

Kitchen Knight

1. _____
2. _____
3. _____

Black Knight

1. _____
2. _____
3. _____

III. Characters: List and briefly describe the main characters in this legend.

_____
_____
_____
_____

IV. Rewrite this legend. Be sure to:

○ Include and underline all of the vocabulary words.
○ Write at least three separate paragraphs.
○ Include the following additional requirements.

_____
_____
_____

Beaumains, the Knight of the Kitchen - Part 3

I

And when they had gone some days' journey they came upon a knight clad all in green who rode toward them. And he called to the damsel, "Is it my brother the Black Knight that I see with thee?"

"Alack," cried she, "it is not thy brother, but a kitchen knave who hath slain him through some evil chance."

When the Green Knight heard these words, he picked up a green horn and blew on it three notes. Immediately there appeared three fair maidens clad in green. And these dressed him in green armor and brought him a green horse and a spear.

"Now, fellow," cried the Green Knight, "I am ready to do battle with thee." And he flew at Sir Beaumains.

Forthwith they thrust at each other with their spears, mighty blows and fierce. And afterwards they came upon their feet and fought furiously with their swords, and in a long time the fight was not over.

"For shame, Green Knight," cried the damsel, "that thou fightest so long with a kitchen knave who hath the odor of meats yet upon him!" When the Green Knight heard this speech, he was angry anew, and anew he ran at Sir Beaumains; and with a fierce thrust he struck at him and brake his shield in twain.

But Sir Beaumains repaid the blow with one as fierce and followed it with a buffet upon the helmet which sent the Green Knight to his knees. Then the Green Knight prayed for mercy, for he perceived that he stood near to his death.

"Nay," said Sir Beaumains, "withhold thy prayer, Green Knight, for there is nothing that will win me to have mercy upon thee, save only if this damsel petition me for thy life."

Quoth the damsel, "I will never petition thee, kitchen knight!"

"Then shall the Green Knight die!" said Sir Beaumains.

The Green Knight prayed again, "My life shall be at thy service and the lives of thirty knights whom I command."

Said Sir Beaumains, "Thy words avail thee nothing. I will spare thee only on the petition of this maid."

Then the Green Knight besought the damsel that she would petition for him.

"Shall I petition to a kitchen knave?" asked she with high chin.

"Nay," said the Green Knight, "I warrant this is no kitchen knave but a right noble knight."

Yet the damsel stood pouting.

Then made Sir Beaumains a movement to unlace the helmet of the Green Knight as if to slay him.

"Hold!" cried the maid. "I am loth that the Green Knight should perish. I pray thee spare him."

And immediately the knight Beaumains held back his hand and spared the Green Knight.

And that night they abode at the Green Knight's castle, which was near, and enjoyed good fare. The next morning the Green Knight accompanied them some distance, and at parting he told Beaumains that he and his thirty knights would do service when and where he might desire. Thereupon Beaumains told him that he must go and yield himself and his knights to King Arthur, and this the Green Knight promised to do.

II

Then when they had left the lands of the Green Knight, the damsel again began to gibe at Sir Beaumains, saying: " Think not that I esteem thee better for this adventure with the Green Knight. For thou shalt, ere this quest be ended, meet one worse than he. Wherefore, I counsel thee to say farewell and go."

Sir Beaumains replied, "Cease thine idle words! Hast thou not yet learnt that I will not leave thee till this quest be accomplished?"

And they rode on till they came to the lands of Sir Persaunt of Ind, and with him also Sir Beaumains did battle and had victory. And Sir Persaunt promised the service of one hundred knights.

And having passed the night at his castle, they went on; but the damsel chided no more, for she began to perceive how valiant a knight was this Sir Beaumains, and she believed he was, in spite of all, of noble blood.

Thus she remained silent, ashamed of her former speech; and in this wise they drew near to the castle of the lady, Dame Lyones, round which a siege was laid.

"Now are we come to the perilous adventure," said the damsel; "for yonder is the castle of the Lady. Alas, Sir Knight, I would thou hadst not come as far as this, for thou shalt surely be vanquished by the Red Knight of the Reed Lands."

"Nay," said Sir Beaumains, "fear not for me. Willingly I took this adventure upon me, and right willingly I carry it to its end. If I speed well, I relieve that most noble lady whom the Red Knight of the Reed Lands thus persecuteth. If I fall, I die as becomes a knight."

In a little while, when they had passed through a fair forest, they came upon a plain, and in the distance was a high castle with many tents about it. And as they rode under some withered trees by the edge of the forest, they saw, hanging by their necks from the bare boughs, many goodly knights in armor with their shields and swords hung before them.

At this shameful sight Beaumains checked his horse and asked, "What means this?"

"Fair sir," said Linet, "abate not your cheer at this dreadful sight, for ye have need now of all your courage. These dead knights are those who have come against the Red Knight trying to rescue my sister from his power. But the tyrant knight hath overcome them and slain them thus shamefully by hanging."

"Now Heaven aid me," said Beaumains, "for this is a most unknightly custom, and well doth that knight deserve death."

With that they came to a sycamore tree which stood alone in the plain, and on it was hung a great horn of elephant bone.

"Fair sir, ye must blow that horn if ye wish to do battle with the Red Knight. But, sir," went on the lady quickly and caught at Beaumains' arm that lifted the horn, "be ye not overbold. It is said that the Red Knight's force increaseth to the strength of seven men until it is noon. Wait, therefore, until noon shall be past, and his strength shall diminish."

"Nay, nay," said Beaumains, "speak not thus to me. I will assail him however mighty he be."

Therewith he lifted the horn and blew so great a blast that instantly knights came in a great press from the tents, and people looked out from the walls and windows of the castle.

III

Then came the Red Knight riding down upon him. That was fire that flew from his eyes, red fire, and his horse was blood-red and his armor and his spear and so was his shield. And they met in a little valley that was near to the castle so that all might behold the encounter.

Now the Lady Lyones looked out of the window, and she was wondrous fair and gentler than her sister. Then she beheld the knight Sir Beaumains, who fought the Red Knight with his spear, giving him mighty blows; and she thought she had never beheld so goodly a knight.

And as she watched, the knights brake their spears. And immediately they leapt from their horses and, seizing their swords, ran at one another. They fought on and all were astonished, for there was never a knight had so long withstood the Red Knight of the Reed Lands.

And when they had rested awhile, they fell to again; and they were like fierce lions in the fight.

Now when the encounter had lasted for a great time longer, Sir Beaumains struck the Red Knight so heavy a blow that all cried out who witnessed it. Then was the Red Knight wroth, and suddenly he smote Beaumain's sword from his hand and dealt him a buffet that sent him over.

Then cried lady Linet, "Sir Beaumains, Sir Beaumains, my sister weepeth and watcheth; fail her not in this fight!"

And no sooner had Sir Beaumains heard the cry than he was upon his feet, and despite the Red Knight he ran for his sword and seized it. And with a mighty strength that came suddenly upon him he smote the Red Knight so that the Red Knight sank to his knees and then was thrust grovelling to the ground.

Beaumains leaped astride him and cut the fastenings of his helm. Then the Red Knight shrieked for mercy.

"Thou recreant and coward!" said Beaumains. "Did not any of those knights that thou hast hung cry to thee for mercy? What pity and what mercy didst thou give them? And thou deservest none from me, nor from any man!"

With that he slew him at a stroke, and the people in the castle cried out with joy.

Then for ten days the Lady Linet made Beaumains rest him in the Red Knight's tent, while she tended his many sore wounds. But ever Beaumains desired to go into the castle to see the Lady Lyones, but his hurts forbade him.

On the eleventh day he would no longer be denied, but, having armed himself, he rode up to the castle gate. But as he came thither he saw many armed men who pulled up the drawbridge before him so that he should not enter. Therewith he saw a knight at a window who called to him.

"Fair sir, I am Sir Gringamor, brother to the Lady Lyones," said the knight. "I will that ye enter not yet. We know that you have proved yourself a bold and brave fighter, but we know not who you are. Therefore unless you tell me your name and kindred, I may not suffer my sister to see you."

Then came a sweet voice crying in tears, and Sir Beaumains saw the tender face of the Lady Lyones at the window. "My brave knight, think not ill of me, for this is none of my will, for my pleasure is denied in my own castle by my overcareful brother. I love thee, sir knight, whatsoever thou art, for I feel that thou art as good a man as any lady might love."

Saying these words, the lady sobbed as if her heart would break, and she was led away by her women.

With that Beaumains' heart smote him, and he was resolved to reveal his name and lineage for the sake of the dear lady. But even as he thought this, he was aware of a party of knights coming towards him from the plain, and soon he recognized that they were of the company of King Arthur's Round Table.

And the foremost knight, who bore his helm in his hand, rode forward to him, crying: "Gareth, Gareth, my brother, how hast thou deceived us all?"

Then did Sir Beaumains clasp the other's hand right warmly, for this was his own brother, Sir Gaheris, sent from King Arthur to bring him home. And when Sir Gringamor knew of the coming of these knights, he bade the drawbridge to be lowered, and in a little while the knights were being welcomed in the hall.

"Sir Gringamor," said Sir Gaheris, "I find that I come at a lucky chance for the happiness of my brother. Already the fame of his brave deeds has reached King Arthur, for the knights he hath overcome have put themselves in the mercy of the king."

"Sir Knight of the Round Table," said Sir Gringamor, "tell me who is this brave knight that will not say his name?"

"He is Sir Gareth, my brother, the youngest son of the King of Orkney," replied Sir Gaheris, "and fit for the highest lady in the land. He hath played this trick upon us all to test us. We did not know him, for he hath grown up to manhood while we have been long away from home. But ever he hath had an adventurous and witty mind."

"Sir, I thank you," said Sir Gringamor, and, taking Sir Gareth by the hand, he led him into the bower where sat the Lady Lyones, who sprang to meet Sir Gareth. To her Sir Gringamor told all that he had heard and then left Sir Gareth to tell her more of himself

And in a little while, at the court of King Arthur, they were married. And Linet was wedded at the same time to Sir Gaheris. For though the Lady Linet was sharp of tongue, she was of a good heart and well beloved of all who knew her well.

Beaumains, the Knight of the Kitchen – Part 3

Name: _____

I. Vocabulary: Underline the following words in the legend. Define each word and use it in a short sentence below.

○ alack: _____

○ buffet: _____

○ gibe: _____

○ chided: _____

○ boughs: _____

II. Plot: Write a simple sentence or phrase to describe the main actions that take place in each scene.

Green Knight	Red Knight	Lady Lyones
1. _____	1. _____	1. _____
2. _____	2. _____	2. _____
3. _____	3. _____	3. _____

III. Characters: List and briefly describe the main characters in this legend.

_____

_____

_____

_____

IV. Rewrite this legend. Be sure to:

○ Include and underline all of the vocabulary words.

○ Write at least three separate paragraphs.

○ Include the following additional requirements.

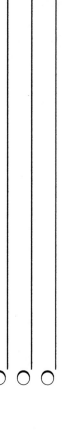

Beowulf and Grendel

News of Grendel

1. Hrothgar builds Heorot.

2. Grendel visits Heorot.

3. Beowulf hears lays.

A Night in Heorot

1. Geates sleep soundly.

2. Beowulf fights Grendel.

3. Grendel escapes wounded.

A Double Revenge

1. Mother rescues arm.

2. Beowulf follows blood.

3. Beowulf kills both.

Beowulf and the Firedrake

Fugitive Burglar

1. Firedrake comes.

2. Gold cup taken.

3. Firedrake takes revenge.

The Fray

1. Beowulf seeks firedrake.

2. Beowulf fights firedrake.

3. Firedrake dies; Beowulf wounded.

A Mighty Mound

1. Treasure brought out.

2. Beowulf addresses followers.

3. Beowulf buried.

Young Roland – Part 1

King among Men

1. Roland awaits the king.

2. Roland is kingly peasant.

3. Page joins friend.

Royal Procession

1. Vanguard draws near.

2. Roland is astonished.

3. Roland heads home.

My Kinsfolk & Myself

1. Mother is King's sister.

2. Mother, Bertha, eloped.

3. Father dies valiantly.

Young Roland – Part 2

A Feast Interrupted

1. Roland enters hall.

2. King questions Roland.

3. Roland "steals" cup.

The Grotto

1. Roland shows prize.

2. Squires bully Roland.

3. Knight intervenes.

Sister Returns

1. King welcomes Bertha.

2. King forgives Bertha.

3. Roland becomes knight.

A Roland for an Oliver

Paris Thanksgiving

1. Charlemagne holds feast.

2. Gerard comes for fief.

3. Gerard rebels.

Siege

1. Charlemagne lays siege.

2. Pagans attack France.

3. Single combat decides quarrel.

I am Conquered

1. Roland fights Red.

2. Fight lasts hours.

3. Roland discovers Oliver.

The Death of Roland – Part 1

Proposal from the King

1. Charlemagne fights Spain.

2. Marsilas promises baptism.

3. Marsilas promises hostages.

Charlemagne's Answer

1. Council is divided.

2. Roland suggests Ganelon.

3. Ganelon betrays Roland.

Traitorous Plots

1. Charlemagne offers half.

2. Marsilas fumes then consents.

3. Ganelon outlines treachery.

The Death of Roland – Part 2

Lo, the Drums!

1. Ganelon suggests Roland.

2. Charlemagne leaves Roland.

3. The heathen approach.

Bold Words and Looks

1. The heathen attack.

2. The French fight valiantly.

3. Roland sounds horn.

Three Blasts

1. Charlemagne mistakes then hears.

2. Peers suffer greatly.

3. Roland prays and dies.

How Oliver Fought for France and the Faith

Mouth Full of Words

1. Fierabras mocks knights.

2. No knights volunteer.

3. Charlemagne argues with Roland.

Throbbing Wounds

1. Oliver craves favor.

2. Favor is granted.

3. Oliver gives ultimatum.

Generous Recompense

1. Oliver fights Fierabras.

2. Fierabras offers clemency.

3. Oliver uses "Baptism."

Balmung and Greyfell

Wonderful Smith

1. Prince Siegfried grows up.

2. Siegfried is sent to work.

3. Regin teaches smithwork.

Balmung is Forged

1. Regin makes swords.

2. Siegfried reforges Balmung.

3. Balmung splits anvil.

Greyfell is Chosen

1. Siegfried seeks fame.

2. Gripir gives horse.

3. Odin chooses Greyfell.

The Curse of the Gold

Oddar the Otter

1. Asa-folk visit mid-world.

2. Loki kills two.

3. Hreidmar sets ransom.

Lo, it Grew!

1. Loki catches Andvari.

2. Andvari pronounces curse.

3. Ring covers hair.

Fateful Ring

1. Loki repeats curse.

2. Hreidmar is transformed.

3. Fafnir is transformed.

Fafnir, the Dragon

Glittering Heath

1. Siegfried and Regin seek adventure.

2. Both reach Glittering Heath.

3. Regin stays back.

The Terror

1. Boatman gives advice.

2. Siegfried digs hole.

3. Siegfried slays Fafnir.

Place of Blood

1. Odin's birds warn.

2. Regin is transformed.

3. Siegfried leaves Balmung and Regin.

In Nibelung Land

Hoard Discovered

1. Siegfried finds brothers.

2. Brothers explain hoard.

3. Siegfried gets Balmung.

Curious Workmanship

1. Siegfried divides treasure.

2. One ring remains.

3. Brothers die of lust.

A Tarnkappe

1. Elves come for battle.

2. Siegfried snatches Tarnkappe.

3. Alberich is overcome.

Siegfried's Arrival in Burgundy

Rumors of Kriemhild

1. Boy grows up.

2. Siegfried seeks Kriemhild.

3. Siegfried visits Gunther.

A Wonderful Knight

1. Siegfried takes Tarnkappe.

2. Siegfried bathes in blood.

3. Single combat proposed.

Danes & Saxons Invade

1. Corps is chosen.

2. Siegfried captures Kings.

3. Siegfried woos Kriemhild.

Gunther and Brunhild

Queen of Iceland

1. Gunther seeks Brunhild.

2. Three contests held.

3. Siegfried aids Gunther.

An odd Nuptual

1. Foul play anticipated.

2. Brunhild regretfully follows.

3. Two couples marry.

The Taming of Brunhild

1. Brunhild incapacitates Gunther.

2. Gunther tells Siegfried.

3. Fabulous strength is lost.

The Death of Siegfried

"After You"

1. Kriemhild comes to visit.

2. Brunhild starts fight.

3. Insults fly about.

Assassination at the Spring

1. Siegfried called to aid.

2. Kriemhild sews cross.

3. Hagen drives spear.

Days of Mourning

1. Hagen fails test.

2. Kriemhild summons Nibelungs.

3. Hagen steals and sinks gold.

St. George and the Dragon

Loathsome Bird	Bitter Weeping	Believe in God
1. King loves Cleodolinda.	1. Sheep are gone.	1. St. George arrives.
2. Poisonous dragon appears.	2. Dragon requires children.	2. St. George fights dragon.
3. Dragon requires sheep.	3. Cleodolinda is chosen.	3. Cleodolinda leads dragon.

The Miracle of the Sword in the Stone – Part 1

First Born Son	Black Looks	With One Hand
1. Merlin aids Uther.	1. Uther names Arthur.	1. Tournament is held.
2. Uther gives Arthur.	2. Archbishop gathers Lords.	2. Arthur returns for Kay's sword.
3. Lords seek throne.	3. Sword in stone appears.	3. Arthur pulls from stone.

The Miracle of the Sword in the Stone – Part 2

On God's Book	Holidays	The True King
1. Kay lies to Ector.	1. Arthur draws on 12th day.	1. Commoners cry "Arthur."
2. Ector seeks truth.	2. Draws on Candlemas.	2. Eleven kings refuse.
3. Arthur hears of adoption.	3. Draws on Easter and Penecost.	3. Arthur is knighted and crowned.

The Sword Excalibur

Coronation Feast

1. All attend coronation.

2. Eleven refuse gifts.

3. Men prepare for battle.

Excalibur

1. Merlin shows lake.

2. Lady makes deal.

3. Arthur takes sword.

Thirty Torches

1. The battle begins.

2. Arthur fights valiantly.

3. Rebels are defeated.

Sir Gawain's Marriage

What Women Desire

1. Arthur is beaten.

2. A deal is struck.

3. Women want what?

Loathly Lady

1. Arthur "finds" answer.

2. Arthur remembers promise.

3. Gawain volunteers.

Double Charm

1. Disguise is lifted.

2. Gawain gives will.

3. Charms are dissolved.

Beaumains, Knight of the Kitchen – Part 1

Pentecost

1. Arthur feasts at Pentecost.

2. Three men arrive.

3. One requests gifts.

"Fair Hands"

1. Man asks hospitality.

2. Kay assigns kitchen work.

3. Beaumains cheerfully submits.

Reed Lands

1. Damsel comes at Pentecost.

2. Beaumains asks boons.

3. Damsel is wroth.

Beaumains, Knight of the Kitchen – Part 2

No Quarrel with Thee	Kitchen Knight	Black Knight
1.Beaumains rides off.	1.Beaumains slays plunderers.	1.Damsel requests pity.
2.Kay is injured.	2.Damsel upbraids knight.	2.Beaumains slays Black Knight.
3.Lancelot and Beaumains tie.	3.Beaumains slays two knights.	3.Beaumains takes armor and lance.

Beaumains, Knight of the Kitchen – Part 3

Green Knight	Red Knight	Lady Lyones
1.Beaumains fights Green Knight.	1.Damsel mocks Beaumains.	1.Beaumains sounds horn.
2.Beaumains wins fight.	2.Beaumains conquers Red Knight.	2.Beaumains conquers Red Knight.
3.Damsel pleads for life.	3.Damsel chides no more.	3.Beaumains marries sister.